The Oliver Wendell Holmes Lectures
are delivered annually at the Harvard Law School
under a fund established out of a legacy
to the Law School from Justice Holmes.
L. C. B. Gower was the Holmes lecturer
in November and December 1966.

The Crimes of Politics
Political Dimensions of Criminal Justice

Francis A. Allen

Harvard University Press   Cambridge, Massachusetts   1974

To Susan, Neil, and Roberta
The Winter's Tale, act 3, scene 3

Preface

The problems discussed in this book in some sense reflect concerns that I have pursued throughout most of my professional life. The closing years of the 1960s, however, brought these interests into clearer focus and placed them in a different context. Between 1966 and 1971 I served as Dean of the University of Michigan Law School. The period was one in which opinions polarized and political tumult prevailed. No educational administrator could have been totally oblivious of the issues posed by these developments, for they created problems demanding his attention day by day, and sometimes hour by hour. These issues perhaps had a special significance for a law dean, particularly one who had been professionally concerned with problems of public order and with the role of law in achieving the domestic tranquillity and liberty that our constitutional fathers had conceived as objects of the American political system.

I am grateful to the Harvard Law School for its invitation to deliver the Oliver Wendell Holmes Lectures in the academic year 1972–73. The lectures provided an occasion and inducement to organize my thoughts about both personal and national experiences during the past decade. The contents of this book, severely abridged, were presented as the Holmes Lectures in Cambridge on March 13–15, 1973. Mrs. Allen and I express our warm appreciation to Dean Albert M. Sacks and to the faculty and staff of the Harvard Law School for their kindness and hospitality during what was for us an altogether pleasant and satisfying visit. I wish to thank the John Simon Guggenheim Memorial Foundation for the award of a fellowship in 1971–72, and the University of Michigan for the grant of a sabbatical leave during the same period. I am also grateful to the William W. Cook Fund of the University of Michigan Law School for a research grant in the summer of 1972. All of this financial assistance provided time for study and eliminated the necessity for a drastic departure from a standard of living that I can hardly describe as lavish, but to which I have become accustomed.

It is never possible to give full acknowledgment of one's intellectual indebtedness to others. This is true both because there are so many persons—colleagues, students, friends, and family— who deserve recognition, and because to a significant but indeterminate degree one is unconscious of his debts. Nevertheless, three friends and scholars must be mentioned. I have relied heavily on their work and counsel over the years, and while I was preparing these lectures, each provided assistance and inspiration of a value that it would be imprudent to reveal. They are Norval Morris of the University of Chicago Law School, Hans W. Mattick of the Chicago Circle Campus, University of Illinois, and Yale Kamisar of the University of Michigan Law School. In addition, I have had the great advantage of the research conducted by Dr. Vera Bolgàr into Continental law and practice in the area of political crimes. I warmly appreciate this assistance and hope that Dr. Bolgàr will organize her findings into a survey and analysis of this aspect of government policy in Western Europe since the Second World War. Such a study in English would fill an important need.

The production of a book, even of modest size, places a heavy burden on secretarial services. I especially appreciate the help provided by Mrs. Ann LaVaque, director of secretarial services at the University of Michigan Law School, and Mrs. Carole London, my secretary.

And then there is my wife. Authors commonly profess in prefatory statements an appreciation for their spouses, often in phrases such as: "I have been working on this volume fourteen hours a day for the past ten years. Never once during that long and arduous labor did I hear a word of complaint pass the lips of my wife." I have often suspected that such statements are to be taken as evidence more of the author's fictional powers than of factual reporting. In any event, June is not like that. After I have been for some time in the semicomatose state that writing produces in me, she is very likely to say, "That's enough." John Milton may have been right when he wrote, "They also serve who only stand and wait," but it is an observation that produces no resonance in my wife's Irish soul. The time has come to acknowledge that, again and as usual, she is correct. It is not necessary to spend *every* waking hour thinking about the next sentence. In fact, the final product may be improved if one is a little less compulsive about his work. I should also acknowledge her remarkably accurate and rapid understanding of the human impact of complex social problems. To the extent that my work has failed to grasp this human dimension, the failure is my own. When it has revealed such perception, the contribution is largely hers. There are, of course, other acknowledgments owed to her, but I had best find other ways to express them.

Contents

The Crimes of Politics
Political Dimensions of Criminal Justice

1. Of Scholars, Crime, and Politics

The present century has given no cause to dispute Aristotle's description of man as "by nature a political animal." Man's political propensities arise, says Aristotle, from the gift of speech. This unique endowment confers on man the power to elucidate distinctions between the expedient and inexpedient, the just and the unjust, good and evil.[1] Because the political arts accrue from endowments both fundamental and specifically human, all forms of human association, beginning with the family, reveal political characteristics; and all ages of human history may fairly be seen as ages of politics. To assert that politics stems from a common fund of human traits, however, is not to deny the remarkable diversity in the forms and modes of political behavior in different cultures and at different times and places. Nor is it to deny that, over time, the politics of state and nation intrudes into the consciousness and lives of men in very different ways, and possesses for them very different significances. Surely the twentieth century is one of those periods in which politics has gained ascendancy in the thoughts and lives of men to an extraordinary degree. However this period's achievements are finally assessed, and whatever else it is seen to be, the twentieth century will be recalled as, perhaps preeminently, an age of politics.

In such an age, political movements produce great events in the lives of men; but equally important, the thoughts and feelings of individuals are profoundly affected by political attachments and assumptions. The very pervasiveness of this political coloration of man's sensibility tends in some measure to exclude it from his consciousness, just as any other everpresent element in his life is not likely to be noticed until events intrude and coerce his attention. Today people are highly receptive to political analyses and explanations over a broad spectrum of human experience, explanations that at other times might more readily have been expressed in the language not of politics, but of science, theology, or philosophy. If it is assumed that a test of the temper of an age is the kinds of explanations that persons spontaneously accept as persuasive, there will be no difficulty in identifying the political orientation of the modern era.

Evidence of a political orientation in broad areas of contemporary American life turns up in unexpected places. For example, many books are currently being published bearing titles beginning with the words "The Politics of." *The Politics of Upheaval* by Arthur Schlesinger, Jr., is a case in point. It may come as a surprise, however, to discover just how attractive these words have proved to those who write and publish. A cursory check of the card catalog of a large university library revealed no less than 241 book titles beginning with "The Politics of." Although one of these books was published as long ago as 1886, over two-thirds were published after 1964. These titles run the alphabetical gamut from *The Politics of Accommodation* to *The Politics of Zoning.* In between one encounters books bearing the titles *The Politics of Scarcity* and *The Politics of Affluence, of Assimilation* and *of Untouchability, of Conscience* and *of Compromise; The Politics of Hope, of Despair,* and *of Doomsday; of Ecstasy* and *of Hysteria; The Politics of the Unpolitical* and *of Experience; The Politics of King Lear, of John F. Kennedy, of the Universe,* and *of God.*[2]

There are more sober ways to demonstrate the imperialistic tendency of politics in our time—its tendency, that is, to encompass and dominate the various areas of human thought and activity. The modern emphasis given in ethics and theology to interpersonal relations, to the "I–thou," as contrasted to more solitary virtues and preoccupations, provides one example. The impact of politics on literature and aesthetics is palpable and unmistakable. Before mid-century George Orwell wrote:

> The invasion of literature by politics was bound to happen. It must have happened, even if the special problem of totalitarianism had never

2

arisen, because we have developed a sort of compunction which our grandparents did not have, an awareness of the enormous injustice and misery of the world, and a guilt-stricken feeling that one ought to be doing something about it, which makes a purely aesthetic attitude toward life impossible. No one, now, could devote himself to literature as single-mindedly as Joyce or Henry James.[3]

The testimony of Albert Camus is consistent with this view:

> In the midst of such a din the writer cannot hope to remain aloof in order to pursue the reflections and images that are dear to him. Until the present moment, remaining aloof has always been possible in history. When someone did not approve he could always keep silent or talk of something else. Today everything is changed and even silence has dangerous implications. The moment that abstaining from choice is looked upon as choice and punished and praised as such, the artist is willy-nilly impressed into service.[4]

The involvement of government policy and political ideology in contemporary physical science and social science is also an established fact. In the 1960s, for example, there developed a widespread concern, based on sound evidence, that agencies of the federal government were secretly funding research congenial to government policy. The concern became sufficiently insistent to induce President Lyndon B. Johnson in March 1967 to issue a policy statement containing the following declaration: "No federal agency shall provide any covert financial assistance or support, direct or indirect, to any of the nation's educational or private voluntary organizations. This policy specifically applies to all foreign activities of such organizations and it reaffirms present policy with respect to domestic activities." Several months later an American anthropologist issued a volume, predictably entitled *Politics of Social Research,* in which he stated: "Social research of whatever kind occurs in a political environment. Directly or indirectly political decisions, ideologies, and relationships are involved, nationally and internationally . . . Political decisions often determine the amount and kind of research undertaken, and the results of research may be used for political purposes that are good or ill." [5]

Not all the consequences of this age of politics have proved benign. To use a phrase quoted by E. M. Forster, this century has too often seen political movements erect "a pyramid of appetites on a foundation of stupidity," and in so doing they have induced the sleep of reason that brings forth monsters.[6] Even those who have escaped involvement in the worst of these horrors have sometimes found the modern temper uncongenial. The malaise of young people today stems in part from their difficulty in keeping group involvements and commitments at arm's length in order to provide for themselves an adequate living space.

Among the institutions that lend themselves most readily to political interpretation are the agencies of criminal justice. The criminal law, courts, and prisons are instruments of government, created and funded by government, and administered by public functionaries. The maintenance of public order is widely identified as a basic purpose of government, to which end the public force is regularly employed. Law enforcement policy has long been a staple of partisan polemics in the United States, and a widespread conviction that governments are failing to honor their basic commitment to secure life, limb, and possessions from criminal injury can shake the foundations of political power and threaten the existence of government regimes.[7] Moreover, American constitutional history has emphasized the necessity of limiting powers exercised by systems of criminal justice to the safeguarding of basic political values. Many provisions of the Bill of Rights are derived directly from seventeenth- and eighteenth-century English political experience, including the prosecution of political offenders. More recent history adds further illumination of these relations. Many Americans, while growing to maturity, observed the rise of European totalitarian regimes and were impressed by the awesome capacities of such societies to subvert the agencies of justice and order to the purposes of party and state, and thereby to destroy or render ineffective competing human and political values. The world and this nation since the Second World War have provided further illustrations of a similar subversion.

Thus, whether viewed from the perspective of its origins, its functions, or its consequences, the system of criminal justice appears to be a natural, even inevitable, subject for political analysis; indeed, political interpretations of criminal justice are today at high tide. Yet a political interpretation of criminal justice was slow to develop in the immediate American postwar era, despite the political orientation of intellectual currents in general. The prevailing attitudes of the immediate postwar period are suggested by four textbooks that were widely used in college criminology courses during the 1950s. No adverse judgment of their quality is implied in the remark that none of them undertakes a consistent view of the system of criminal justice as an instrumentality of state power or as a process having the potential for either fulfilling or impairing basic political values. One of the books contains no index reference to politics or politicians. Two others restrict themselves in this area to problems of bribery and the gross corruption of police, courts, and prisons. The fourth includes one paragraph of just over a hundred words on the "penalizing of acts believed to threaten government." The last three sentences of the paragraph assert: "Our Department of Justice has a Civil Liberties Bureau. Its very existence indicates a government interest in the protection of civil liberties the violation of which may be crime. The tense world situation, however, has complicated the activities of the Bureau." [8]

It can fairly be said that the political dimensions of criminal justice were not of primary concern to most of those professionally or academically involved in the study and administration of American criminal justice during the years preceding the mid-1960s. The main interests and commitments of American criminology at that time were nevertheless many and varied, covering a broad spectrum of concerns, most of which are still viable. Among the most important commitments of those involved with problems of crime and corrections was commitment to the rehabilitative ideal.[9]

Adherents of the rehabilitative ideal place their faith in the scientific understanding of human behavior, and some foresee the scientific control of human behavior.[10] This understanding and capacity for control make possible the therapeutic treatment of convicted persons. Such treatment seeks both to effect changes in the behavior of offenders in the interests of their happiness and welfare and to strengthen the social defense by eliminating criminal propensities in the individuals treated. This complex of ideas has had a significant impact on the modern world; in varying degrees, most people are adherents of the rehabilitative ideal. Many of the characteristic reforms in criminal justice over the past century, including probation, parole, and the juvenile court, are products of these ideas, as are many of the ameliorating efforts within the penal system. It is clear that the rehabilitative ideal responds to something fundamental in the modern temper; and it is equally clear that the treatment afforded convicted offenders suffers from a scarcity of genuine, thoroughgoing rehabilitative programs in correctional systems.

There is very little in the rehabilitative ideal that is explicitly political. Indeed, its concentration on the individual deviant and his unique psychic difficulties produces an apparently apolitical emphasis. Yet any considered position on the problems of criminal justice will, if implemented, have a distinctive social and political impact and produce its fair share of unintended consequences. This is as true of a view that gives overriding importance to the therapeutic functions of the justice system as it is of any other view. In short, there is a "politics" of the rehabilitative ideal, despite the fact that until recently most of those devoted to the therapeutic orientation were largely unconscious of its social and political significance. The principal feature of the rehabilitative ideal as a political phenomenon is that its influence has been predominantly (but not inevitably) conservative, tending to sustain and buttress the status quo. This is true for a number of reasons.

When the interests of criminology are concentrated on a single part of the criminal justice process, other problems of the system tend to be neglected, and many institutional practices, deserving examination, are accepted without challenge. If most scientific attention is devoted to the therapeutic treatment of convicted offenders, small interest will be manifested in the legal definitions of criminal behavior or in the process by which persons are identified, selected, and designated as criminal offenders. The convicted criminal offender will tend to be accepted as a given. Yet the questions neglected by or excluded from scientific inquiry—such as what kinds of behavior should be deemed criminal, or whether the system of criminal justice is administered fairly and evenly for all segments of the population—are issues that became of critical importance in the late 1960s, not only for the system of justice but for all of American society.

The tendency of the rehabilitative ideal, however, is to go beyond the scientific neglect of important issues or even the inhibition of needed reforms because of this neglect. The rehabilitative ideal, by concentrating attention on the internal pathologies of individual offenders, expresses a bias against views that attribute the causes of criminality more largely to broad social factors and, therefore, call for a significant reordering of social arrangements in response.

Tendencies of the rehabilitative ideal may be compared with those of other familiar attitudes or systems of thought relating to crime and criminal justice. A half-century ago and more, a eugenics movement strongly influenced American popular and academic thought about crime and its control. The movement reflected a sense of excitement in the rediscovery of Mendelian genetics and the continuing influence of Darwinian biology. Except in a few areas of specialized concern, the eugenics movement also exerted an adverse influence on broad social reform. If one is permitted to believe that crime, mental disease, and even poverty are primarily products of defective genes rather than of the malfunctioning of institutions, one may with good conscience avoid the difficult tasks of altering existing social arrangements or even of thinking seriously about them.[11] Perhaps more striking are the characteristics common to both the rehabilitative ideal and the popular, moralistic attitudes associated with the strict ''law and order'' position. In many important respects this is a curious pairing, for nothing is more calculated to provoke derision and contempt in strict law-enforcement disciples than the assertion that many criminals are in some sense ''ill'' and require professional treatment for their ''cure.'' Nevertheless, both views locate the causes of criminality in the internal condition of the individual offender, and both advocate measures

7

designed to alter that condition. As Kai Erikson put it: "We may learn to think of such people as 'sick' rather than 'reprobate' but a single logic governs both of these labels, for they imply that nothing less than an important change of heart, a spiritual conversion or a clinical cure, can eliminate that inner seed which leads one to behave in a deviant fashion." [12]

Finally, experience has shown that the administration of therapy by correctional systems, in those comparatively infrequent instances when genuine therapeutic efforts are made, tends to be supportive of the system and to discourage protest and criticism. There is a pervasive ambiguity about the ends of therapy—a problem of determining which is the illness and which is the cure. Ordinarily, the adjustment and accommodation of the person treated to the system's requirements become the practical objectives of the institutional therapeutic effort. This is obviously a value-laden choice, and in recent years politically radical inmates have not been slow to perceive the fact. Two convicted war resisters recently asserted: "We feel that each political prisoner must decide for himself whether it is best to 'adjust' to, or resist, prison authority. If his choice is the latter, he ought to steer clear of the Mental Hygiene Clinic." [13]

This attempt to describe the mood and content of some of the dominant strains in American thought about crime and corrections in the immediate postwar years contains the usual deficiencies associated with efforts to compress complex movements of thought within a brief compass. It would be patently erroneous to imply that in those years no thought was given to the political implications of criminal law and the administration of penal justice. It was in that period, after all, that the foundations were laid in the Supreme Court of the United States for the luxuriant growth of doctrines relating to the rights and immunities of persons caught up in state or federal criminal processes.[14] In those same years, American public law was absorbed in defining basic First Amendment rights of free speech and association as affected by criminal prosecutions of those charged with politically subversive activities.[15] Nor were all students of criminal justice either unaware of or unconcerned with the largely unarticulated

political implications of the rehabilitative ideal. A critique en-
compassing those implications emerged, amplified by lawyers,
sociologists, and psychiatrists.[16] Despite these exceptions and
qualifications, however, the dominant interests of American
criminological thought in the years leading to the mid-1960s did
not include a view of criminal justice as an instrumentality of
governmental power directed, on occasion, to the achievement
of political objectives that were adverse to the interests of some
members of the community. There was little disposition to
launch a fundamental assault on the legitimacy of the system;
most of its aspects were accepted, ignored, or not seriously
challenged. Criticism in general was aimed at the corruptions
and inefficiencies of institutional practices, not at ultimate purposes and goals. Indeed, the trained criminologist was likely to
argue that he could achieve the system's purposes more effectively and humanely if only given the authority to do so.

Although it is sometimes said that there are no discontinuities
in history—no abrupt turns or sudden changes—there are nevertheless times when thought and events manage to negotiate
rather precipitous curves within comparatively short intervals.
The decade of the 1960s, especially its closing years, was one of
these. Rapid, even dramatic, changes occurred in academic
thought about crime and criminal justice, resulting in an emphasis and content quite different from that which had characterized
earlier tendencies. Whatever the intellectual ancestry of contemporary trends in criminological thought, certain historical events
in the 1960s had an immediate and critical impact on their development. These events included, first, the prolonging of the Vietnam War and the popular opposition it engendered and, second,
the rise of black militancy and a new assertiveness on the part of
other ethnic groups. Related to these occurrences, but indepen-
dently important, was the emergence of a youth culture asserting
values and behavior in conflict with established conventions at
various points. All three of these developments directed attention
to social conflict and nourished an acidulous skepticism toward
earlier assumptions of social and political consensus. All
three developments involved groups that were asserting values

and goals in some measure antagonistic to those of established political authority, and all three gave rise to serious concerns about the uses of state power, including power administered through the system of criminal justice, as an instrumentality for the repression of deviant political attitudes and behavior.

These events contributed to a number of distinctive attitudes in academic thought about crime and criminal justice. One of the most striking is the breaking down of certain practical inhibitions in the study of crime and justice, and the application of skeptical analysis to areas formerly ignored or neglected. No longer are the justice system and the presence of the convicted offender accepted merely as givens. An acute, sometimes almost morbid, sensitivity is expressed about the purposes to which new knowledge may be placed by official agencies. This suspicion is frequently communicated as a concern that scientific investigators may be "co-opted" by the system, by which is meant the entrapment of investigators and technicians into serving institutional ends that they regard as improper or dubious.[17] This unease has extended to some modern therapists. In 1971 a well-known psychiatrist wrote: "Now I am plagued with doubt . . . whether I behaved morally in carrying out psychotherapy in prison at all . . . By participating in the punishment process, even as a healer, I loaned a certain credibility to the existing correctional system." [18] Thus, there has been a declaration of intellectual independence from the system being studied and, in some cases, a decision to withdraw support and assistance from it.

Closely related to the liberation achieved by some criminologists from the purposes and assumptions of the system is the broadening of areas of research and inquiry. The modern investigator may continue to be interested in discovering why convicted offenders violate criminal regulations, but he is just as likely to concern himself with a very different question, namely, whether there is any rational basis for the regulations said to be violated. Shortly after World War II, Hermann Mannheim complained, "Hardly ever do we pause for a moment to examine critically the contents of that very law the existence of which alone makes it possible for the individual to offend against it." [19] This criticism is less telling today. Concern about the administration of drug laws and the impact of their enforcement on young people has led to inquiry into the assumptions on which these laws rest. Disorders prompted by political disaffection have led to speculation about the bases of legal obligation and have raised issues, both substantive and procedural, concerning the imposition of sanctions in such cases. A substantial and diversified literature on law enforcement has emerged, as have studies on other aspects of institutional behavior. In short, the areas of criminal law and its administration, which traditionally were at the periphery of criminological interest in this country, have come to be seen as matters of crucial and central concern.[20]

Most striking of these new trends, however, and influencing them all, is the emergence of an explicit political consciousness, a concern with political values, and an inclination to conceive of the issues of crime and criminal justice as problems in the use and abuse of political power.[21] Jerome Skolnick epitomized these attitudes when, in a published interview, he said, "I see less and less of a distinction between political science as a discipline and sociology of crime, or criminology as a discipline." [22] This identification of criminology with political science by a sociologist is paralleled by what appears to be a new and broader interest in the administration of criminal justice by researchers in the political science departments of American universities.

The mood and movement of American social thought during the last decade has been compatible to these tendencies and attitudes. They are in no sense confined to the study of crime and criminal justice, but characterize work in fields far removed from criminological inquiry. It is apparent that these manifestations reflect a common modern experience. One of the most persistent characteristics of the modern mood is revealed in the widespread expressions of concern about the social consequences of new knowledge and in the determination of investigators to encompass these issues within the ambit of their interests and obligations. Such concern is of course not new in Western thought. In his *Lettres Persanes,* Montesquieu gave

11

expression to the eighteenth century unease accompanying what he called "the ravages of chemistry." "I have not been in Europe long," Rhedi observed to Usbeck, "but I have heard sensible people talk of the ravages of chemistry . . . I tremble, lest in the end people arrive at discovering some secret which will furnish a quicker way of causing men to perish and of destroying entire peoples and nations." [23] The modern concern, however, has enlarged into an altogether different and higher order of magnitude. Although frequently expressed in the social sciences, its most notable statement has occurred within the physical sciences. No doubt it was the release and military application of atomic energy in the 1940s and the continued apprehensions of even more destructive uses in the postwar world that were most influential in creating this pervasive unease; but the impact of the Vietnam War has been hardly less important. The universality of this concern and its intensity go far to establish its validity and, perhaps, its inevitability.

An unfortunate circumstance of human life is that unmixed blessings are in chronically short supply. One may fairly assert that contemporary academic thought about crime and criminal justice is livelier, broader, and more self-conscious than that which preceded it. Yet some of what has been written and spoken by academic criminologists in the past half-decade is also dubious and disconcerting. New constraints on the openness of inquiry are apparent, different from those that characterized the earlier era, but potentially as limiting. Aggressive and unabashed espousals of political ideology on the part of some vocal scholars give rise to serious questions about the relations of personal commitments to the integrity of the scientific enterprise. Occasionally a tendentiousness, a lack of caution and proportion, appears in what is written. In short, one begins to suspect that the process so elegantly described by Isaiah Berlin is being re-enacted: "The history of thought and culture is, as Hegel showed with great brilliance, a changing pattern of great liberating ideas which inevitably turn into suffocating straitjackets, and so stimulate their own destruction by new, emancipating, and at the same time, enslaving conceptions." [24] Perhaps it is an overstatement to assert that modern criminology is in danger of being enslaved by its own emancipation. It seems responsible to suggest, however, that implicit in recent criminological theorizing are certain tendencies which, if not contained, threaten the usefulness and validity of its contributions in the years ahead.

Any intellectual stance breeds its own distinctive pathologies, so perhaps it is not surprising that much of what appears dubious in recent academic thought about crime and its control is closely related to what is most attractive. Legitimate concern about the social and political applications of knowledge is an essential aspect of recent attitudes. Without a considerable infusion of judgment and good sense, however, such concern may result in constraints on inquiry that threaten both its freedom and its capacity to advance the collective well-being. This outcome is most likely to occur in the area of criminology when proposals are made to study techniques of enhancing the efficiency of law enforcement. Some researchers have chosen to avoid such studies and, in some cases, to oppose them. Frequently the ground of opposition is that the police are politically repressive and that to advance the efficiency of law enforcement, therefore, is to render more effective its capacities for political repression. David H. Bayley recently wrote:

The question is even now being asked on several campuses whether money and university facilities should be allocated to the study of the police—let alone the training of them—rather than to the alleviation of basic social problems that would reduce the need for police.

In short, the years of disinterest are over, but the years of productive study may not yet have arrived. Ideological fashions may be no less destructive than professional ones of serious research.[25]

Guarding against the guardians is a complex problem in the best of times; it becomes almost infinitely difficult in a technetronic age. Yet the withholding of systematic knowledge from the system of law enforcement until wholesale social changes can be effected seems less an answer than an abdication. This is true, in part, because of the devastating effect of crime, and the fear of crime, on American life—most particularly on American political life. There is no historical warrant for surprise at discovering that the desire of persons to escape internal violence and disorder may override virtually all countervailing considerations. "Thou shalt not be afraid of any terror by night nor for the arrow that flieth by day," promises the Book of Common Prayer; and those who ignore this basic human aspiration do so at their peril. Fears of law enforcement abuse have sometimes led political liberals and radicals to underestimate the deleterious impact of crime on the lives of persons and even to doubt the reality of the problem.[26] Yet the fact is that the quality of life of millions of persons is debased and the sense of security on which any decent existence depends has been impaired by crime in the streets, in the school, in the parking lot, in the apartment complex. The result has been to encourage a conviction in the public mind that does no service to the cause of liberal reform; namely, that the objectives of reform, and in particular the goals of political and social equality, are unattainable except at the sacrifice of the securities and decencies of life to increasing levels of criminal behavior. The apparent unwillingness or inability of many reformers to contribute to the effectiveness of crime control tends to ensure that law enforcement practice and policy will be vested in those ignorant of or insufficiently concerned with the human and social costs of law enforcement abuse.

The age of politics has given rise to other hazards for criminological inquiry. Not the least of these is what Donald Black called the "confusion of science and policy," a confusion that in some instances renders dubious the characterization of work as scientific.[27] The role of values in scientific inquiry, particularly in social inquiry, is the subject of a large and burgeoning literature. The question presents problems of genuine difficulty, and these complexities have not always been adequately appreciated. In 1860 Thomas Henry Huxley wrote to Charles Kingsley: "Sit down before a fact as a little child, be prepared to give up every preconceived notion, follow humbly wherever and to whatever abysses nature leads, or you shall learn nothing." [28] It would not be easy to formulate a proposition less descriptive of the actual processes of scientific inquiry. The first difficulty inheres in locating the fact before which one is to sit. The process of selection from an infinity of possibilities involves experience, sophistication, and commitments that are the opposite of childlike. Nor does this exhaust the difficulties. There is an increasing awareness of the alarming extent to which what one actually sees and hears is determined by his predispositions.

It is one thing, however, to recognize that drawing the line between fact and opinion strains and sometimes exceeds human capacities. It is quite another to surrender the effort, to ignore the line, and to abandon the search for empirically validated propositions. The point is not to separate the results of genuinely scientific inquiry from public policy. The continuing hope is for a policy amenable to the influence of scientific findings and a social science capable of producing them. Nor should persons who are academic criminologists be barred from full participation in the political polemics of this era and from stating or advocating their value preferences. To present ideology as the product of scientific inquiry, however, raises a very different question. To suffuse value preferences with the aura of scientific discovery is to exploit the substantial confidence in science that still characterizes this age [29] and is an essentially fraudulent procedure. In quality it is hardly different from the exploitation of religious belief in an age of faith by representing existing political arrangements as the product of divine revelation.

For law and lawyers, other aspects of the new tendencies in criminological thought are of more direct concern. Specifically, one might question the potential of the new political awareness for making useful contributions to needed reforms of the criminal law and its institutions. This question can fairly be put even if it is true that law reform and the enlightenment of lawyers do not rank high among the purposes of those producing the new literature.

The question, however, does not lend itself to a single, general answer. Contemporary social theory as it relates to crime and the institutions of justice is characterized by divergent, sometimes contradictory, tendencies. One modern statement may nevertheless be examined for its utility to those concerned with contemporary problems of crime and of social responses to crime. Richard Quinney formulated the following basic propositions:

> Crime is a *definition* of behavior that is conferred on some persons by others. Agents of the law . . . representing segments of a politically organized society, are responsible for formulating and administering criminal law. Persons and behaviors, therefore, become criminal because of the *formulation* and *application* of criminal definitions. Thus, *crime is created.*
> . . . . .
>
> Criminal definitions are formulated according to the interests of those *segments* . . . of society which have the *power* to translate their interests into *public policy* . . . In other words, those who have the ability to have their interests represented in public policy regulate the formulation of criminal definitions.
> . . . . .
>
> Since interests cannot be effectively protected by merely formulating criminal law, enforcement and administration of the law are required. The interests of the powerful, therefore, operate in *applying* criminal definitions.[30]

These assertions are of course not novel. They share an affinity with the literature of realist jurisprudence in the 1920s and 1930s: law is what the legislatures, (or the courts), say it is; and what they say is determined by the dominant interests in the community. Indeed, the propositions have a more ancient lineage, in that justice is again seen as the interest of the stronger.

The familiarity of these propositions, however, should not obscure their contemporary political relevance. Among those committed to the modern politics of dissent, assertions very like Quinney's have been widely adopted as part of a basic operating theory. The reason is that these propositions serve both to describe a view of reality and to provide justification for certain kinds of political action. For groups hostile to existing social arrangements and committed to action that, on occasion, may contravene the criminal law, a view of the law simply as an expression of the interests and power of the socially dominant becomes virtually indispensable to claims of personal justification and moral legitimacy.

For the purposes at hand, however, these propositions are relevant not primarily because of their utility for political activism or even their adequacy as jurisprudential postulates. Rather, the question is whether commitment to the view of the criminal law as a device to achieve the particular interests of the socially powerful is likely to produce significant advances toward new knowledge and valid insights. There is room for initial doubt. Legislators giving consideration to what the law ought to be are not noticeably assisted by being told that the law is what the legislators say it is. Lawyers performing legislative functions, such as code revision, are likely to be surprised and bemused by assertions that, whatever their conscious purposes, they are in fact the instrumentalities of powerful special interests.

There is a large tautological element in Quinney's propositions. The criminal law is formulated and applied by public agencies; in the long run and for the most part, therefore, it may be expected to reflect, or at least not seriously to offend, the views and interests of those capable of influencing public policy. Indeed, on occasion the criminal law may be used directly as a device to attain the political objectives of those possessed of political power. These observations, however, do not carry one far toward understanding the basic power relations of any particular society; and if care is not exercised, they may lead one astray. Individuals and groups who wield political power do so in a bewildering variety of ways and with varying degrees of purpose and consciousness. One way to achieve political objectives is to define certain behaviors as criminal and to penalize those who violate the criminal regulations. Yet there are other less public and sometimes more sinister ways to exercise political power; and a society in which politically dominant elements rely significantly on the processes of criminal justice to achieve their ends is not necessarily less benign than one in which power more frequently eschews legal procedures and proceeds along less visible paths.

This may be one lesson to be derived from the great English state trials in the reigns of the Tudors and the early Stuarts. Paradoxically, the disposition of those monarchs to resort to the criminal law as a device to eliminate enemies of their autocratic

17

regimes may have in the long run contributed to the development of English political liberties. This is true even though the procedures employed in the trials forced the accused into grossly unequal contests with the state, whose results were often drastic and preordained. Not until 1695 was the accused in a treason case granted the statutory right to employ counsel to conduct his defense.[31] The defendant was accorded no privilege to summon witnesses to support his cause. He was not even supplied with a statement of the charges against him until he was in the courtroom on trial for his life.[32] Only rarely did a defendant, assisted by a remarkable quickness of wit or by a more than ordinary ineptitude of the judge and prosecutors, manage to gain acquittal from a courageous jury.[33] No doubt the necessity of providing proof, however light the prosecutor's burden, also at times deterred the exercise of repressive state power against persons believed to be enemies of the regime. Finally, the state trials—although lacking in equity and, (of equal importance), incapable of adequately separating the guilty from the innocent—maintained a tradition that before a man may be condemned as a traitor, he must be shown to be such, and they dramatized the need for procedural reforms that were ultimately effected when circumstances permitted.

Modern experience again suggests that the criminal law is often an ineffectual instrument for achieving the political objectives of those possessed of power. This fact has often been perceived by persons eager to employ state authority for oppressive ends. It is no fortuity that the aggressions against the foreignborn in the Palmer raids of 1919 and 1920 involved use of the administrative processes of deportation rather than the procedures of criminal accusation and trial. A deliberate decision was made by public officials to employ administrative devices because the obligations of proof and the other resistances built into the criminal process incapacitated it for use in such a sweeping program of repression.[34] Even Hitler discovered that courts presided over by judges trained in the assumptions of the law could not be trusted when measures vital to the regime were involved, and in such cases he tended to exercise his autocratic authority

through other channels.[35] This is not intended to suggest that the criminal law is incapable of being used as a device to achieve repressive political objectives. Such use has been made in the past, and similar uses will no doubt occur in the future. It is important to be aware, however, that the choice to exercise political power through the established agencies of criminal justice has often meant a moderation of oppression, not its exacerbation. Such an awareness gives a significantly different coloration to the proposition that the criminal law is the instrumentality of the socially dominant.

There are other reasons to believe that a model of the system of criminal justice based on Quinney's assumptions fails to encompass many important factors. If the criminal law is to be seen primarily as an instrumentality to protect the interests of the socially dominant groups, one cannot but be puzzled by the remarkable insouciance displayed by those groups toward the tasks of crime definition. The history of criminal legislation in this country is a story of unconcern, neglect, and ineptitude. Despite a recent revival of interest in the substantive criminal law as manifested by the production of the Model Penal Code, codification projects in several states, and pending proposals in Congress,[36] what remains most striking about the American penal law is its frequent failure to identify and provide realistic protection for a range of basic social interests, including most especially the interests of the middle class and other groups whom modern critics have identified as the politically dominant segments of American society.

The history of the Anglo-American law of theft is instructive here. In the creation of crimes against property more than anywhere else, one would expect to find the criminal law revealed as reflecting the interest of the affluent and powerful. Such was the view of a not inconsiderable authority, Adam Smith. "Civil government, so far as it is instituted for the security of property," he wrote in *The Wealth of Nations,* "is in reality instituted for the defence of the rich against the poor, or of those who have some property against those who have none at all." This assertion was strikingly echoed in a novel of Joseph Conrad, where Mrs.

19

Verloc, wife of the anarchist agent, said to her mentally retarded brother: "Don't you know what the police are for, Stevie? They are there so that them as have nothing shouldn't take anything away from them who have." [37]

To deny all validity to these statements would demand a good deal of hardihood. The influence of dominant interest groups, of the wealthy and powerful, can be identified throughout the history of theft law all the way back to the Saxon village society with its concern for security from the cattle-raid. [38] Some of this history can fairly be described in the language of class conflict. The proliferation of capital penalties for trivial property crimes in the early years of the industrial revolution reflected in some measure the fears and antagonisms created in the propertied groups by the new working classes being spawned by the factory system. [39] In general, the expansion of theft law doctrine follows the emergence of new and important forms of property as they are given birth by a developing economy.

Yet as often happens when one scrutinizes history more closely, the initially perceived patterns become less clear. The shibboleth that the theft law expresses the interest of the strong appears less useful. Indeed, the least contestable generalization about the law of theft is that it is always anachronistic. It lags and has always lagged behind the development of new and sometimes highly important economic interests. The modern criminal law of commercial fraud is only about two centuries old; it emerged long after an acute need had been clearly demonstrated; and it continues to provide imperfect protection for substantial economic interests. Modern legislation and judicial decisions deal inexpertly or not at all with many other property relationships; and efforts to adapt the law to the protection of these interests are frequently frustrated by legislative inertia or hostility. [40] The reason for this persistent failure of propertied groups to achieve more adequate protection for their own interests from the criminal law lies partly in ignorance, professional conservatism, and institutional failure. These are the rocks on which demon theories of history often founder. But there are other reasons why it is misleading to rest with the assertion that

the law of theft is an instrumentality for protecting the interests of the powerful. The statement suggests a unity of interest among those possessing some measure of political influence, which is demonstrably at war with reality. This divergence from reality is particularly acute in a pluralistic society where economic power and political influence are broadly dispersed among numerous and contending groups. The interests of the landed proprietor are hardly closer to those of the industrial entrepreneur than are the employer's interests to those of the industrial employee. The interests of the politically powerful investing groups are not the same as of those offering corporate securities for sale. Thus, the ultimate resolution involves an intricate vectoring of a great variety of forces, a complexity hardly hinted at by the assertion that the criminal law is the tool of the politically dominant.

Moving from crime definition to the practice of law enforcement, one discovers less equivocal support for the view of criminal justice as a tool of the powerful. American history affords frequent instances of the use of the police and militia as shock troops in political and industrial disputes. Words like Homestead, Pullman, the Memorial Day Massacre are evocative. To this list might be added more recent instances, such as Chicago in 1968 and the bridge at Selma.

Nevertheless, a view of the police simply as an instrumentality of the wealthy bourgeoisie in a Marxist class struggle scarcely comports with the facts, present or past. More seriously, it fails to give adequate definition to the growing American police problem, that is, the capacity of police organizations in some urban localities as well as the federal level to resist and neutralize direction from civil authority. Closely related is the apparent ability of the rank and file in many police organizations to evade effective control from the upper administrative echelons of these organizations. On occasion, the "interests" that the police appear to be most assiduously serving are not those dictated by oligarchic power groups in the community or by legitimate civil authority, but interests defined by the police themselves. The degree to which the police, like the military, are capable of constituting a "third force" in American society, with interests and power significantly distinct from other politicial groups, is only beginning to be apprehended. Any formula that diverts attention from such facts renders a dangerous disservice.[41]

The sober work of American criminological inquiry has been moving forward during the past decade, and a growing methodological sophistication is displayed in the new research. Moreover, an increasing number of young scholars in the law schools are expressing dissatisfaction with society's abysmal ignorance of the consequences of legal sanctions. These young scholars have discovered that for the most part those who create and apply penal sanctions literally do not know what they are doing, and have hardly begun to find out. Some students are consciously equipping themselves to narrow the range of ignorance.

The discovery of the political dimensions of criminal justice by investigators in university departments outside the law schools is also commendable. Because of the nature of penal sanctions, the interests that the system of criminal justice is called on to protect, and because of the system being an arm of government and a channel for the exercise of state power, criminal justice is inherently and inescapably political. It was the failure to perceive these facts that rendered much prior scholarship in the field irrelevant and sometimes perilous to the maintenance of essential political values. Basic human interests are today, as in the past, threatened by the exertion of state power through the agencies of penal justice; in consequence, it is of first importance that this realization be reflected in the scholarship. The nature of some of the perils is well symbolized by the incarceration of the Soviet dissentients in mental hospitals and the equating of political and cultural dissent with mental disorder. One cannot afford to discount these events simply as typical excesses of a foreign totalitarian society. From time to time the assumptions underlying the Soviet practices have been given explicit articulation in the literature of mental health movements in the Western world.[42] In addition, such disturbing phenomena as the serious consideration of brain surgery for the treatment for certain vio-

22

lent prisoners and persons involuntarily confined in mental institutions, and the dubious use of tranquilizing drugs as devices for the control of fractious inmates, suggests that Americans do not lack for problems of their own.[43].

Nevertheless, the new political awareness that characterizes much modern academic thought about crime and penal justice has not always contributed to sense or to the liberation of thought from artificial constraints. It is one thing to identify the political dimensions of criminal justice and to give them full and appropriate consideration. It is quite another to assume that all vital issues in the field are resolved by a political analysis. And it is still another to conceive of scientific criminology as an appropriate vehicle for the dissemination of political ideology. Among the losses associated with these latter courses is that they diminish the capacity of systematic thought to contribute marginal gains to the decency and good sense of the processes through which societies identify disturbing and dangerous behavior and take measures against it. It is on this margin that criminology has in the past made its most constructive contributions. However disappointing to wider ambitions, I suspect that this will prove to be true in the future as well.

In an age of politics, scholars are the prototypal fiddlers on the roof. The scholar, like the fiddler, must perform; but also like the fiddler, he must maintain his balance. The first cannot be achieved without the second. What is worse, the scholar is called upon to cling to his perch in a tempest of contending values that often reaches gale level. Unlike the fiddler, however, he may fall off the roof without knowing it. The scholar's lot in these days is not an easy one. But it probably never was.

2. Misadventures of a Concept

During the decade of the sixties many more students and commentators than in preceding years were closely scrutinizing the political dimensions of criminal justice in search of insight and understanding. Some, but by no means all, of such political analyses were themselves political acts, producing and intended to produce political consequences. Much territory, however, remains to be explored. Even persons most disposed to perceive the penal law as politics would be likely to concede that some parts are more political than others. There are, after all, differences between treason and chicken theft; and this is true even when the chickens are owned by the state and the theft occurs on a government-operated collective farm.

Probably there has always been an acute popular awareness of the qualitative differences that separate ordinary criminal acts from those intended to overturn a government or regime, or those directly challenging the exercise of power by agencies possessed of political authority. It is this perception that for almost four centuries has kept alive Sir John Harrington's epigram:

> Treason doth never prosper; What's the reason?
> Why, if it prosper, none dare call it treason.[1]

The precise point of this apothegm has also been made in the literature of other nations. Thus, Montesquieu told of a king who, "having defeated and imprisoned a prince who disputed the crown with him, began to reproach him for infidelity and treachery. 'It was decided only a moment ago,' said the unfortunate prince, 'which of us was the traitor.' "[2]

Despite the fact that this nation was founded by persons who were accused of treason and, (had the outcome of their struggle been different), might have died as traitors, the concept of "political crime" has played no significant part in American legal history and hardly a greater role in American political history. Except in one important legal area, the United States, along with most other nations in the Anglo-American legal tradition, recognizes no concept of political crime that identifies a category of offenses possessing distinctive doctrinal significance or requiring application of distinctive modes of treatment to convicted offenders. Perhaps more surprising than the neglect of the political crime concept in the formal law is the fact that only infrequently have references to "political" offenders and "political" prisoners formed any significant part of public discussions in the United States. One of these rare periods encompassed the years immediately following the Civil War, when questions of measures to be taken against those who adhered to the Southern cause, including the amnesties to be awarded, attracted the interest and concern of a large public. More recently, but now largely forgotten, was the acrimonious public debate that broke out concerning the continued imprisonment of persons convicted of obstructing the military effort in the First World War. The flavor of this controversy was conveyed by an address of Attorney General Harry M. Daugherty in 1921 to the American Bar Association, where he observed:

In this country there is now being disseminated an extensive propaganda to dignify the crimes committed by many persons who are now in prison for disloyal conduct or for obstructing or hindering the Government in prosecuting the war with Germany, and, by means of such propaganda to create a public sentiment not only to have such criminals freed, but to have this general doctrine of political offenses recognized as a part of our domestic law, the purpose being, when the doctrine is once recognized, to enable criminals and those in sympathy with them to continue such opposition to law and order with impunity . . . In order that the general character of this propaganda may be understood, it should be stated that these propagandists term all the anarchists, I.W.W.'s, and socialists, who have been convicted of law violation, idealists, and heroes of conscience, and demand their release on the ground that the acts of these persons are political offenses merely.[3]

The third of these periods of public discussion is the present time, when political movements have produced acts in contravention of the criminal law, most particularly those acts associated with resistance to the Vietnam War and related to black activism.

Probably the most striking and incontestable characteristic of the political crime concept is its elusiveness. The problem of definition is well illustrated in the one significant area of American law in which the courts have been required to grapple with the political crime concept—in cases, that is, in which fugitives are seeking to avoid extradition to answer criminal charges in foreign nations.[4] The principle that one charged with a political offense is not subject to extradition, now routinely asserted in treaties of extradition [5] and sometimes expressed in municipal laws, is in its origins a product of nineteenth century liberalism. The principle reflected a growing popular sympathy for acts of resistance to autocratic governmental regimes and public indignation at the spectacle of one's own government cooperating to return such a resister to the control of an oppressive regime, whose retaliation against him might often be expected to exceed all humane limits. The inexpediency of the asylum state's becoming actively involved through the processes of extradition in the internal political struggles of another country was also apparent, especially in cases in which there might be substantial uncertainty whether the cause represented by the fugitive or that of the requesting government was likely in the end to succeed.[6]

To express the general principle and to speculate about its origins and purposes present no particular difficulties. To define what a political offense is, however, has proved to be an infinitely more demanding undertaking. Indeed, no generally valid definition has yet been formulated. "Up to the present day," wrote one commentator, "all attempts to formulate a satisfactory conception of the term have failed, and the reason of the thing will, probably, forever exclude the possibility of finding a satisfactory definition." [7] Crimes that contain political ingredients distribute themselves on a spectrum ranging from so-called absolute political crimes—high treason and the like—to ordinary-appearing criminal acts that may disguise political motivations, or criminal acts producing political consequences but committed without political motivation. The actual definitions accepted in the various countries adhering to the political offense limitation have proved fluid and, more often than not, have reflected political conditions in the asylum states and in the international community.

The indignation and fears produced by acts of political terror perpetrated by anarchists and other revolutionary groups in the last half of the nineteenth century produced an impact tending to narrow the scope of the limitation. In 1854 an attempt was made to assassinate Napoleon III by blowing up the train on which he was traveling. When France requested Belgium to render up the accused, the courts of the latter country felt compelled to refuse on the ground that their law forbade the surrender of political criminals. In response to this situation, Belgium in 1856 amended its extradition law by enactment of the so-called *attentat* clause, which excluded the murder of the head of a foreign government or a member of his family from the definition of political crime. This exception was widely adopted by other states and, in some instances, was expanded to cover other sorts of homicide.[8]

In the years since the Second World War, the scope of the political offense limitation on extradition has been subjected to various and opposing influences. In the aftermath of the war there arose strong impulses to facilitate the extradition of those accused of "crimes against humanity." No doubt, crimes against humanity differ from political offenses in ways other than that the former tend to be committed by persons possessed of political or military authority, whereas the latter are often directed against the exercise of political authority. Nevertheless, these categories are not always clearly separated, and nice problems involving their distinction can arise.[9] The tendency of the crimes-against-humanity doctrine was in some measure to constrict the immunities from extradition. Perhaps more than counterbalancing this tendency, however, was the change in the character of persons seeking asylum in the Western democracies in

27

the years immediately before and after World War II. Tens of thousands of refugees fled, first from Nazi oppression, and later from countries in which Communist regimes had gained power. Even when charged with offenses, these persons had less the look of political activists than of victims of authoritarian persecution. Such circumstances evoked sympathy and support for a vigorous doctrine of immunity from extradition.[10]

Today a new era of political terrorism has emerged. One of the costs of terrorism is that it tends to destroy the impulse for a liberal response to political opposition and to impair the doctrines that express this impulse and make it effective. What is most disturbing about modern acts of political terror—the hijackings, the kidnapings, the bombings, and the machine gunnings—is their patent disregard of the interests and rights of the innocent, indeed, their systematic exploitation of these interests to extort political benefits. The international community must give new attention to the means that individuals employ to achieve political objectives.[11] The claims of common humanity now require a closer, more critical look at the doctrines of the political offense and the practice of political asylum in some of their modern applications.

The utility of the political offense concept as a moderating influence in the administration of criminal justice has been demonstrated in areas other than international extradition. Certain Western European countries and other nations whose legal systems are based on Continental models extended the concept into their domestic law.[12] This development, like those in the extradition field, was in its origins a consequence of an emerging political liberalism in the nineteenth century. In its simplest forms the doctrine was one of mitigation of penalties in behalf of those found to have committed certain political offenses or delicts. ''The political offender is not like other offenders; he violates the criminal law because he combats the particular political regime that applies the law,'' asserted a French treatise on the criminal law. Characteristically, continued the treatise, ''the legislator in a liberal regime is indulgent toward political offenders.'' [13] The political offender, it is assumed, is motivated by

28

purposes that are clearly more elevated than those manifested by common criminals. His acts reveal a concern for human happiness and welfare that is in striking contrast to the self-serving goals of those guilty of ordinary offenses against persons and property.

Because the political offender is significantly different from, and morally superior to, those who commit common crimes, it follows that the penalties imposed on him should reflect these differences by being less rigorous and debasing, and by manifesting the state's perception of the dignity of the conscientious law violator. Moreover, the nature of the political offender's motives causes him to be less amenable to the deterrent threat of criminal punishment.[14] To impose harsh penalties on the nondeterrable is both futile and cruel. The doctrine is one of mitigation, not of excuse or justification. The political offense is not to be overlooked, but the necessary restraints on the offender should interfere with the normal pattern of his life as little as possible. After the Munich putsch of 1923, for example, Adolph Hitler, as a political offender, was awarded the special form of confinement known as *Festungshaft* at Landsberg Prison, and under this mild regime he found the conditions favorable for writing *Mein Kampf*.[15]

Whatever may be the ultimate judgment about the realism and feasibility of this application of the political offense concept, it has an unquestioned ethical appeal. Moreover, for reasons that perhaps are not wholly selfish, this version of the political offense doctrine coincides with the expectations of the political offender; and when those expectations are disappointed, (as very often occurs), a sense of injustice is produced in the offender and his supporters. This is well illustrated by the bitter reflections of Brendan Behan in his autobiography, *Borstal Boy*. While still an adolescent, Behan, then an I.R.A. activist, was apprehended in England and placed in penal confinement. As his release drew near, he observed, "Well, fair is fair, and . . . I knew what he meant and it was the usual hypocrisy of the English not giving anyone political treatment and then being able to say that alone among the empires she had no political prisoners.'' Similar reactions could doubtless be collected from among American war resisters and other ''prisoners of conscience'' during the decade of the sixties.[16]

The doctrine of political crime, however, is by nature fragile; its emergence and survival depend on the presence of certain benign attitudes toward political opposition, even when that opposition takes the form of law violation. These attitudes, in turn, reflect an awareness of ideological division in society, a perception that the government and its laws do not speak for the entire national community. At the same time, such attitudes reveal a confidence that, although the political opposition may threaten the tenure of parliamentary governments, it is not directed against the fundamental assumptions and arrangements of society. Quite obviously this kind of tolerance and confidence have not flourished in the twentieth century world. The fanaticism and brutalities of this century's politics have not proved congenial to doctrines of leniency for political opponents; in fact, the political offense doctrine appears to be in a state of decline or to have disappeared altogether in many of the nations that in earlier periods gave it recognition.[17] Moreover, the perception of political offenders as constituting a group different in character from other law violators does not ensure that those who commit political crimes are treated more leniently or accorded greater dignity than other offenders. On the contrary, the result may be the imposition of harsher, more rigorous treatment on political offenders; indeed, in the years since the First World War this has probably been the more usual consequence.

Nothing resembling the Continental doctrine of political offenses has gained recognition in American law or, so far as I have been able to determine, in that of other nations of the Anglo-American legal system. This does not mean that recognition of political motivations in the behavior of offenders has played no part in the actual operation of American legal institutions. On occasion this awareness may influence the behavior of police, prosecutors, judges, and juries. It may also affect the treatment meted out to convicted offenders in correctional institutions and the exercise of executive clemency. At times the system has shown greater leniency for such violators; but by no means has this always been true, especially in times of war and of great public excitement.[18] These practices, however, whether tending to mitigation or to greater severity, have never been encompassed in explicit legal doctrine.

Perhaps the closest approach in the United States to a doctrine of political crime is the body of constitutional law that applies limitations to governmental intrusion into the protected areas of speech, press, and association.[19] In one way or another most discussions of political crime, its definition and repression, encounter the values given protection by the First Amendment. A vigorous and adaptable body of constitutional doctrine in these areas is certainly one of the most important contributions that the legal order can bring to the political life of a liberal society. Yet there may be disadvantages in the American tendency to relegate all concerns in this field to the processes of constitutional adjudication. Some problems of legislative and judicial policy are, after all, not well adapted to constitutional consideration; others are not readily justiciable in any form. Here as elsewhere in the polity, a decision favorable to the constitutional validity of a legislative measure or an executive order has tended to terminate discussion and thought, both in and out of legislatures. American legislative action intended to deter varieties of politically motivated behavior is often characterized by dubious estimates of the effectiveness of enacted proposals, inadequate consideration of the range of consequences that may be anticipated from their enactment, and inadequate concern for the quality of the draftsmanship. Although these deficiencies are the product of more than a fixation on constitutional jurisprudence, that fixation has made an important contribution.

Why the United States has not adapted the political offense concept to the purposes of domestic penal law remains an interesting question for speculation. A partial answer may be suggested by the vigorous court-administered doctrines of First Amendment law, which have perhaps resulted in more limited efforts at legislative control of politically motivated behavior than have those of similar purpose in some Continental countries

31

that historically have included the political offense concept in their internal law.[20] To the extent that American penal legislation is narrower in scope, there is correspondingly less occasion for recognizing formal doctrines of mitigation in behalf of political offenders. This explanation, however, appears dubious at best; certainly it does not explain the peculiarly vehement rejection of the political offense concept by many American lawyers and public figures whenever the concept has been advanced in public controversies. At such times the opinion is sometimes expressed that the presence of political motives in law violation constitutes, if anything, an aggravation of the offense rather than a mitigation. Warren Harding, while a presidential candidate in 1920, found it prudent to strike this note:

> I wish no one to misunderstand me, and therefore, I will say as plainly as I can that for my part I can see no essential difference between ordinary crimes on the one hand and political crimes and political prisoners on the other hand. If there is a distinction, surely it is not a distinction which favors political crimes or political prisoners. The thief, or any ordinary criminal, is surely less a menace to those things which we hold dear than the man or woman who conspires to destroy our American institutions.[21]

Among lawyers, talk of "political crime" is typically greeted with incredulity. A distinguished attorney once observed to me, "A lawyer talks about political crime when he has nothing else to offer for the defense." Recently an American judge remarked, "I happen to be one who believes that there are no such things as political trials in the United States." [22]

There thus appears to be evidence of a basic incompatibility in the ways in which Americans have traditionally regarded their society and their law, on the one hand, and the concept of political offense, on the other. The American constitutional tradition reveals a realistic awareness that the powers of government may be abused at the expense of the people's liberties; and the assertion that the government which governs least governs best, while rarely manifested in the practices of either major party when in control of the national administration, still is capable of producing favorable response in many American citizens.

32

Despite this suspicion of government, or perhaps in part because of it, and despite the disruptions of American society in the 1960s and 1970s, it is plainly neither easy nor congenial for most Americans to conceive of their government as an enemy or adversary. Nor have they found it easy to avoid antipathy for persons acting on a contrary assumption, or to credit those persons' claims of a justification for law violation on grounds of morality and conscience. This disposition is no doubt related to the fact that the American republic has not experienced a bloody revolution which pitted class against class, it has not been oppressed by an autocratic or totalitarian government, and it has not suffered the rule of a foreign conqueror or of a puppet regime installed by a foreign conqueror.[23]

In recent years a school of American historians has arisen dedicated not only to the proposition that violence is as American as cherry pie but also apparently to the view that this nation has subsisted largely on a diet of cherry pie. This new scholarly emphasis perhaps contributes a needed corrective to former views of the American past.[24] Yet the corrective may produce its own serious distortions if it causes one to lose sight of the fact that for most of American history the greater proportion of the population has regarded American society and its institutions as supportive of humane values, and that among those sharing this faith have been many who were poor and disadvantaged. Most American citizens, however casual they may be toward their obligations to obey the law, have not conceived of the law as a body of commands imposed by a hostile ruling class. Rather, they have looked upon the law as the product of a democratic process in which they are participants. Those accepting this view can hardly have been unaware that the American federation encompasses a formidable array of regions, groups, and factions whose interests are often in conflict and who engage in vigorous struggle for political influence. Yet the very diversity of this pluralism has led many to believe that they are not doomed to occupy a minority position on all important issues, and that there is reason to hope that today's minority might be tomorrow's majority. In short, most Americans have not conceived of the law and the institutions of justice as creations alien to them and their vital interests. On the contrary, their hostility is likely to be directed toward those who challenge the authority of the law, and who appear thereby to jeopardize the elaborate system of privileges and restraints on which the law and the political institutions of a pluralistic society are based.

One characteristic of the crisis that has afflicted American life in the years since the Second World War is that these widely held perceptions of the nature and purposes of American society have dimmed. How profoundly they have been altered and how lasting the changes will prove are not yet wholly apparent; but that an erosion of confidence has occurred and that it has not been confined to intellectual and literary circles or to the dispossessed can hardly be doubted. Many Americans suffered shock at the first realization that significantly large segments of the population now doubt the goals of American life and the means employed to achieve them. In many instances the shock turned to trauma when it was discovered that these segments included their own children. An awareness that traditional concepts of one's society are being subjected to fundamental challenge can be a stimulus for new thought and constructive reexamination of what previously was accepted largely as given. Unfortunately, however, other responses may more often be produced, particularly when the rejection of traditional perceptions is accompanied by aggressive rhetoric and symbolic behavior. There has arisen in this country an intense nostalgia for the old consensus. Whether the consensus was ever as complete as now recalled is almost beside the point. What is of alarming significance for criminal justice is the apparent willingness of some that the state should attempt, through coercion, to restore a consensus that in earlier times arose spontaneously.

It is against this background that current controversies about political crime in the United States must be appraised. Angry charges that certain criminal proceedings are "political prosecutions" or that certain persons penally confined are "political prisoners," and angry responses that such things do not and cannot exist in American society, reveal significant divergences in contemporary conceptions of the nature and prospects of American life. Quite often these disputes seem centered as much on the symbolic language employed as on the underlying realities. When this occurs, whatever opportunities there might have been to deal rationally with reality are largely forfeited. An area that illustrates these propositions is the field of correction.

Of the multitude of problems demanding prompt, effective public response in the United States, none today is more obvious than the need for fundamental reform of prisons and correctional practices, and few are more important to the quality and stability of American society. The American ''prison problem'' is not a new issue, for its essential dimensions were defined a century ago; and at least since the turn of the century the general directions along which reform must proceed have been apparent to all who have informed themselves about the state of the prisons.[25] The conditions out of which these problems arise, however, have acquired a new virulence; and there is evidence of a broader awareness of these dangers than at any time in the recent past. It is in the prisons that the pathologies of any society are likely to be revealed in their most stark and concentrated form. In an age of political and social protest, the prisons will almost inevitably constitute a focal point of agitation and unrest. This is true, in part, because penal institutions are likely to be among the most vulnerable to valid criticism and the most productive of moral outrage. It may also be true because prisoners, who are among the most alienated and rejected members of society, are sometimes viewed as promising recruits for movements of revolutionary reform.

In the 1930s George Orwell, reflecting on his youthful experiences as a member of the colonial police, wrote:

The Burmese themselves never really recognized our jurisdiction. The thief whom we put in prison did not think of himself as a criminal justly punished, he thought of himself as the victim of a foreign conqueror. The thing that was done to him was merely a wanton meaningless cruelty. His face, behind the stout teak bars of the lock-up and the iron bars of the jail, said so clearly. And unfortunately I had not trained myself to be indifferent to the expression of the human face.[26]

In the literature of American black militancy the colonial analogy figures prominently, and one specific application of the concept has been to view black inmates of penal institutions as "political" prisoners, regardless of the crimes of which they were convicted and imprisoned.[27] How widely this perception has spread or how tenaciously it is held among black prisoners and in the communities from which they come is not clear.[28] As careful an observer as Norval Morris, however, asserted that "we have, possibly for the first time in the world, the emergence in this country of the 'political prisoner' who is not a 'political criminal.' "[29] The proposition has been enlarged to encompass other than black prisoners. The prison population as a whole, it is asserted, is made up of the victims of an oppressive society—of persons who should be regarded less as offenders and more as social or political hostages. Thus, Father Philip Berrigan, commenting on his fellow inmates in a federal prison, wrote: "So we had that common bond with them; in a very wide sense, almost everybody there was a political prisoner. And almost all of them had the firm intention of confronting the system, using the best means at hand."[30]

That these assertions should prove bizarre and incomprehensible to many is inevitable. Whatever plausibility modern Americans may find in theories of the social causation of crime, most are not likely to find the concept of the political prisoner persuasive as applied to those who inflict serious harms on others for motives of personal gain, pleasure, or vengeance, and whose victims are drawn largely from the same social strata as the prisoners themselves. Nor is this skepticism surprising or unsupportable. Among those most vitally interested in academic explanations of criminal behavior are persons who have been convicted of serious crimes. This is true both because of the injury to self-esteem engendered by a felony conviction and because of the human desire of the prisoner to discover the explanations that are least threatening to his conception of himself.[31] Thus, prisoners constitute a prime market for criminological theory; and it is remarkable how quickly they acquire a working knowledge of the substance and vocabulary of current intellectual fashions. In this respect the Officer Kropke song in Leonard Bernstein's *West Side Story* is entirely sound. According to the delinquents, their mothers are junkies and their fathers are drunks. The song is mocking and the mood sardonic; but the point is that the young delinquents in fact know what the psychiatrist, the judge, and the social worker are saying to explain their behavior. These explanations are of great importance because, knowing what assumptions underlie the approach of their social surrogates, the delinquents, in or out of prison, are placed in a better position to resist the system arrayed against them or to manipulate it to their own advantage. The academic explanations are also important because they may weigh less heavily on the delinquent and provide defenses, however, fragile, to his self-esteem. Thus, when the individual hears himself described as a political prisoner by persons outside the institution or by politically conscious fellow prisoners, he may be expected to listen intently, and in some cases he may find the label useful and congenial.

The reality seeking expression in the language of "political prisoner" cannot be safely dismissed as part of a common sense rejection of the vocabulary employed. One measure of the seriousness of the present crises is the demonstrated incapacity of common sense—of the conventional wisdom—to supply adequate understanding of the problems faced or to suggest means through which wise responses can be made. The common sense of the community may prove sufficient when it arises out of a commonality of experiences and circumstances, which in turn give life to widely shared views about behavior and events. Unfortunately, the most pressing and difficult issues have emerged precisely in those areas in which this commonality of experience, and hence of understanding and outlook, are lacking. In these matters, the common sense of the suburb is not the common sense of the ghetto. Nor, because each has in some sense lived in a different world, is the common sense of the old identical to that of the young. This does not mean, as members of groups defined by race, age, or gender sometimes argue, that none but members of these groups can comprehend their problems. A more profound pessimism can hardly be imagined, for such assertions overlook and depreciate one of the most important of the specifically human traits, on which most education is founded, namely, the capacity of men to learn through vicarious, as opposed to direct, experience.

It is well, therefore, for those who have not shared the black experience or the experience of acute poverty and deprivation to seek out the reality that underlies the increasing use of the political prisoner characterization of those imprisoned for crimes involving behavior not ordinarily conceived of as political. It is a somber reality. The facts have been documented so frequently as to require no new corroboration.[32] The social reality is that black residents of deprived areas of large cities constitute the group most likely to be caught up in the processes of criminal justice; that they suffer substantial comparative disadvantages at virtually every stage of the criminal process, from apprehension and arrest to the treatment dispensed in jails and correctional institutions; and that upon release they become the least marketable members of a labor force which, at best, suffers serious disadvantages in the competition for employment. These disabilities are in some measure explicitly racial and, in other respects, the products of poverty. In some instances the discriminations are unconsciously meted out; but in others they are quite consciously imposed. So long as these facts exist, blackness and poverty will determine in a substantial, if indeterminate, number of cases those who are to be incarcerated in American prisons. Inevitably, these facts will prove increasingly intolerable to politically conscious persons among such groups and will encourage a perception of prisoners less as criminals than as victims of the larger society.

Nevertheless, the language employed, as well as the reality it seeks to describe, is important. Unfortunately there is reason to suspect that the political prisoner label may sometimes obstruct efforts to alter the realities that give rise to the label. One of the limiting circumstances encountered by movements of institutional reform is that needed changes require at least the tacit support of a great many persons who possess no very profound understanding of the issues involved and who, partly for this reason, lack any very intense commitment to the goals of reform. Language like "political prisoner" may often divert such persons from the hard tasks of social reconstruction to disputes about the symbolism employed by protesting groups. This may be especially true of prison reform, where the public has displayed an almost Freudian resistance to awareness of the long-standing and widely publicized conditions existing in the correctional systems.

Still other losses may be suffered because of the use of such language. Allegations of the deepening radicalization of prison inmates provide convenient explanations for correctional officials when outbreaks of violence, like the grim fiasco at Attica, occur in the institutions. The lurid language of prison protest lends credence to these explanations and, in some cases, may permit deplorable and remediable conditions in the prisons to escape public scrutiny. Thus, the warden at Attica, testifying before a legislative committee, was reported in the press as having "minimized accounts of prisoner grievances and placed much of the blame on 'Marxists and Maoists.' " The commissioner of corrections, however, testified that he possessed "no evidence to document a Communist conspiracy or a revolutionary conspiracy" and concluded that "there had to be more underlying factors." [33]

The vocabulary of protest may perform useful and even necessary functions for protesting groups. It may contribute to a consciousness of individual identity, to cohesiveness, and to the collective morale. Yet it can delay or defeat amelioration of the conditions prompting protest. As Margaret Mead wrote, "Effective, rapid evolutionary change, in which no one is guillotined and no one is forced into exile, depends on the cooperation of a large number of those in power with the dispossessed who are seeking power." [34] Moderation in the behavior and vocabulary of protesting groups might reasonably appear most likely to create conditions favorable for this necessary cooperation. But this is true only when those possessing power are capable of responding to moderation. Too often in the clamor of the times it is only the raucous, the belligerent, and the overdrawn who are heard.

Any effort to trace the career of the political offense concept must ultimately deal with the question of its utility. Does the idea contribute usefully to contemporary thought about criminal justice? Does it advance the creation of a coherent penal policy, and might it benefit the practical administration of criminal justice? Most American lawyers and judges have not thought so, and there is little reason to suppose that their judgment will be abandoned soon. The reasons for this skepticism and hostility go beyond the fact that the political offense concept is not a part of the legal tradition in which American lawyers are schooled, and that the concept, in at least some of its forms, has appeared incompatible with firmly held assumptions about the nature and purposes of American society. In addition, variations of the political offense concept have been employed in some of the most extreme instances of semantic abuse in the modern era. Nor is the propagandist's attraction to its use difficult to comprehend, for labels like "political trial" and "political prisoner" evoke shattering recollections in twentieth century man. They bring to mind the "ghastly theater" of the Moscow purge trials in 1937, Arthur Koestler's *Darkness at Noon,* concentration camps, torture, firing squads, genocide, and the never-ending migrations of political refugees. The propagandist's business is the use of the "sanguinary simile." He achieves his desired objective by inducing acceptance of labels that encompass widely disparate forms of reality under the same rubric, so as to confuse the morally benign, or morally neutral, or morally dubious with the deplorable and the malignant. The purpose of the propagandist is to terminate analysis and reflection and to recruit emotion in the service of whatever objectives he may wish to promote.[35] Because the political offense concept has been so often and so obviously associated with such efforts, many persons have assumed that it has no legitimate uses.

Rejection of the concept as meaningless because of the abusive uses to which it has often been put may, however, involve the risk of being diverted from a segment of reality that deserves attention and concern. This rejection may in the long run play into the hands of the political propagandist, for the denial that political crimes occur, that political prosecutions are brought, and that political prisoners exist is ultimately indefensible and is itself an obstacle to thought.[36] If by a political trial one means a proceeding motivated in some measure by calculations of the prosecution's effect on government stability, its likely impact on voter behavior, its potential for discrediting a political opponent or cause, and its efficacy in maintaining established values relating to the means that may be employed to effect political change—then, of course, political trials are part of the American system of justice, and they will very likely constitute a part of any alternative system, including those proffered by persons who today make pejorative use of the term. So also do political prisoners exist, at least in the sense of persons incarcerated for behavior directed to political ends but violating the legally defined limits of such behavior or persons who have refused public obligations mandated by the law, and perhaps in other senses as well. These facts can be readily confirmed by observation. Moreover, the labels and classifications associated with the political offense concept are part of the modern argot. Ignored and unanalyzed, they are capable of producing confusion and demoralization.

It is clear that attaching the label "political crime" to a statutory offense does not constitute a reasoned condemnation of the legislative act. Ordinarily the act of classification constitutes only the beginning, not the conclusion, of a necessary process of evaluation. One needs to ask further: Is the behavior that is proscribed and made punishable by the statute protected by constitutional provisions? If not, is the danger that the statute seeks to remove or lessen real or illusory? What range of consequences can reasonably be anticipated from enactment of the legislation and its application in criminal prosecutions? If the danger identified by the statute is real, are there other public responses that might more sensibly be made? Should the danger be ignored, met by efforts of conciliation and accommodation, or responded to by deterrent measures other than criminal sanctions, in the interests of decency or greater effectiveness? Much the same questions can be asked about labels like "political trial" and "political prisoner." Was the person convicted of behavior properly punishable? Was he fairly tried, and are there special problems encountered in providing fair trials for political offenders and making the fact of fairness apparent to the citizenry? Has the convicted offender been decently treated in the penal institutions? Is his confinement consistent with the political values that the government has been delegated to advance, or does his incarceration weaken those values or render them nugatory? None of these questions is answered by simply attaching a label to the person or to the proceedings that resulted in his confinement. Yet any reasoned appraisal of the government's performance requires that answers to these questions be provided.

Nevertheless, most of the disputes involving the political offense concept in recent years have involved the application of labels. One quickly perceives that the acts of defining the concept and of applying it in a particular context may themselves be forms of political action, engaged in or resisted for the purpose of achieving political gains or minimizing political losses. When the political offense concept is employed as a stratagem or a battle cry, one does not expect to derive precise or even intelligible meanings from the terms employed. This confusion of meaning, however, cannot be explained solely by the tactical uses to which the language is put. To a considerable degree it stems from genuine and significant differences in the perceptions and premises of those acting for the state, on the one hand, and of the offender and his supporters, on the other.[37] One striking feature shared by the publicized criminal trials of the late 1960s was the almost unvarying characterization of the prosecution as "political" by the defense and the equally inevitable denial by the government.

This absence of premises common to prosecution and defense is illustrated by the recent case of *Chase v. United States*. At the trial the government was able to establish overwhelmingly that the accused had removed draft records from a selective service office and burned them in an alley behind the building. Four of those criminally charged advanced the defense of "insanity," although, as the court of appeals noted, there was "virtually nothing in the record to suggest that any of the defendants was suf-

42

fering from any legally cognizable mental illness . . . or that they did not fully understand that their conduct was wrong as measured by the standards prescribed by society.'' The defendants offered witnesses to prove that their moral values incapacitated them from comprehending the ''wrongness'' of their law violations and that, therefore, they lacked ''the cognitive capacity to distinguish right and wrong.'' [38] This apparently sardonic effort of the defense to equate moral conviction with insanity in contemporary society was quickly and properly frustrated by the trial and appellate courts. The effort, however, serves as further evidence of the drastically divergent postulates of prosecution and defense in such cases and suggests reasons for the difficulties in defining the political offense concept.

Despite these difficulties, however, the political offense concept is capable of serving useful purposes. Problems of definition need not be insuperable when the concept is employed to identify an area in which to study public policy and its implementation, so as to gain insights that may be useful for the administration of criminal justice. In any event, this use permits a flexibility of definition that cannot be tolerated if the rights of persons in the criminal process are made to depend on the proper formulation of the political offense concept.

Two reasonably distinct categories make up the core of the political crimes classification. In the first category, the political characterization derives from the conduct of the defendant and from the governmental or political interests that are injured by his conduct. The second category encompasses cases in which neither the conduct of the defendant nor the interests injured by him have a distinctly political coloration, but in which the motive of the prosecution is, or is said to be, to achieve some ulterior political objective.

The first of the categories—that of crimes in which the conduct of the defendant is directed to distinctly governmental or political interests—presents fewer conceptual difficulties. Illustrative of it are such offenses as treason, espionage, and sabotage, which expose the nation to the depredations of its external enemies. Also encompassed are offenses of internal subversion and disorder, such as acts of rebellion designed to overthrow the government; assassination of public officials for the purpose of effecting political change, (as contrasted to acts of private vengeance); advocacy of the forcible overthrow of the government; individual or organized resistance, on policial or conscientious grounds, to the exercise by the government of its constitutionally conferred authority; rioting or the instigation of riots for any of these purposes; and acts of symbolic political protest, like those prohibited in the red flag laws of the 1920s and the destruction of draft cards in more recent times.[39] This recital is by no means exhaustive. Perceptions of what interests and motives are "political" are subject to sudden and substantial change. Nor can difficult problems of inclusion and exclusion be avoided. Bribery of public officials and jury tampering, for example, involve injuries to important governmental interests. So long as the purposes of the defendant are to secure a merely personal advantage, however, it seems best to exclude such cases from the political offense concept. In reality, of course, motives are often mixed and may include both private and public ingredients. In these and other cases, the familiar difficulties associated with drawing lines are encountered.

Although controversy and recriminations are characteristically associated with political crime in any of its forms, some of the most intense and persistent public controversies have been inspired by cases in the second category. In these cases the crimes charged are not political by definition. Instead, the offenses alleged may be any one of such felonies as murder, arson, theft, or crimes of sexual immorality. These cases are characterized as political, not because the criminal behavior is alleged to have injured important governmental or political interests, but because the prosecution is instituted, or is widely believed to have been brought, in order to accomplish some ulterior political purpose— to remove a political opponent of the regime, for example, or to discredit a political cause.

Although suspicion that such political motives underlie prosecutions can arise in widely divergent situations, a study of these situations reveals certain patterns. A great many of them, in fact, conform to one of two principal types. The first type involves cases in which the prosecution is attacked on what might be called the theory of the unfounded accusation. The defendant, it is contended, is wholly innocent of trumped-up charges brought by a government seeking political benefit from the defendant's conviction and imprisonment. One of the most important historical examples of such cases was the prosecution of Georgi Dimitrov and his Communist codefendants for burning the Reichstag in 1933, a proceeding that involved a remarkably clumsy and unsuccessful effort by the Nazis to relieve themselves of responsibility and to saddle their political enemies with culpability for the deed.[40] In this country, the case of Sacco and Vanzetti represents for many persons a prime instance of such a case.[41] To judge from foreign newspaper commentary, observers in Western Europe were disposed to view the recent prosecution of Angela Davis in the same light, a view that was widely shared in the United States.[42]

The second type of cases in this broad category reflects what can be called the theory of purposeful discrimination. The defendant may or may not concede that he is guilty of a technical violation of the statute, but he insists that similar violations have been overlooked by the government in the past, and that the prosecution against him has been instituted by the government, not to vindicate the policy of the statute, but to embarrass or incapacitate one whom it regards as politically undesirable. Similar contentions may be made in connection with the sentencing function: the sentence, while within the authorized statutory limits, is more severe than those ordinarily imposed for similar behavior. The difference in treatment is explained on political grounds.

Although these are the cases encompassed most frequently in the political crimes notion, an additional group of cases is involved. This consists of situations in which the accused defines the prosecution as ''political'' because he believes that the effort by the state to punish the behavior in question violates his fundamental rights and the basic political values of the community, or that the methods employed by the state to enforce the law are similarly offensive. Such a case may be included in the political offense concept when the accused and a substantial group of which he is a member demonstrate a willingness vigorously to protest the law and even to resist it. Because of these indicia, today's marijuana law enforcement may be conceived of as falling within the area of political crime.

Although the political motivations of offenders in the United States may affect the actual responses of official agencies in various ways, the political offense concept has not become part of domestic criminal law. Nothing in the American experience, including that of the last decade, suggests that any such formal adaptation is imminent.[43] This is true of doctrines of mitigation patterned on the Continental model, as well as of proposals intended to enhance, or to make more explicit, the jury's power to consider the accused's motives when arriving at its verdict on the criminal charge.[44]

Nevertheless, recent experience with the prosecution of politically motivated behavior has raised serious concern. The gains and social costs associated with this use of the criminal process must be considered, and there is a need to discover what light this experience sheds on the limits of the criminal sanction. More generally, it must be determined whether the emerging patterns of criminal justice promise to nourish basic American political values or threaten their depletion. These large and difficult questions require attention, even though wholly satisfying answers may not be found.

3. Reflections on the Trials of Our Time

Canvassing the various contributions to the literature of political justice, Otto Kirchheimer wrote, "Finally, there are the legal theorists, whose intellectual efforts stand in inverse ratio to their influence on actual practice." Kirchheimer was surely correct in counseling modesty when estimating the impact of academic criticism in this area of public policy. No amount of analysis is likely to deter a government from taking protective measures when it feels that the security of the state is threatened. Mr. Justice Holmes once remarked that detached reflection cannot be demanded in the presence of an uplifted knife.[1] What is true of individuals is, in this respect, also true of political societies. One difference, however, is that societies are perhaps more prone than individuals to apprehend threats when none exist.

The life cycle of legislation in this field tends to encourage lawmaking at those times when rationality and reflection are least likely to be in evidence. Typically, laws proscribing political behavior are enacted in periods of strong public feeling, sometimes bordering on hysteria. Typically, too, such periods, although recurrent, are short-lived. Nothing is so dead as yesterday's red scare; but the veering of public attention away from the subject that earlier produced hysteria weakens the impetus to repeal or modify the legislation passed in a state of public excitement.[2] The result is to confer a kind of immortality on such laws, making some available for continued application by an unobserved bureaucracy, and maintaining all for use in the next recurring period of public agitation. When the next period arrives, not only are the old laws likely to be applied, but they may also stimulate new legislative adventures in repression and crime definition.[3]

The role of academic criticism in this area is peripheral at best. It may nevertheless have some importance. Detached reflection on their experience may diminish the ignorance that condemns societies to relive the past, and may induce or hasten their sober second thoughts, even in periods of public excitement. In short, analysis and reflection will not ensure a policy guided by wisdom, but they can contribute to sophistication. In this field, sophistication may provide a stronger bulwark than wisdom; at least, it may be easier to acquire.

Not only are there difficulties involved in conferring precise or consistent meanings on the political offense concept, but the definition of political crime is itself a political question. This is true both because of the pejorative uses of the label, which have become a common political tactic, and because of the genuine differences in views of what is considered political among the various contending groups in an age of social controversy. Thus, for some, the issue of enforcing laws prohibiting the possession, use, and sale of marijuana has no political overtones over than what may be involved in bolstering the resolve of police agencies to enforce vigorously and efficiently the enacted legislation. For others, however, these laws and their enforcement are seen as forcible invasions by the state of personal privacy and individual volition, and as an assault on a group culture that encompasses specific political attitudes on a variety of issues. It is entirely clear that no definition of political crime is adequate to contain all the meanings that have been assigned the term in recent years or to serve all the purposes to which the label may be applied.

The first point to be made about political crime is that it is a common feature of organized political societies. Use of the criminal process is not the only way that governments seek to protect important political interests; indeed, it is in no sense the most important way. Nevertheless, despite whatever self-denying ordinances a political society may impose on itself in the form of constitutional restraints on state power, and regardless of how cautious the exercise of government discretion may be, no society has forsworn all resort to the processes of criminal justice to protect its political institutions and values. This remarkable unanimity of conviction about the utility and necessity of criminal sanctions confers at least a presumptive validity on the practice, however deplorable and indefensible these uses of the criminal process have proved in great numbers of particular cases. Certainly, the legal propriety of defining and prosecuting political crimes has been recognized in the United States since the beginning of its national life. The American history of political crime begins with the definition of treason in the constitutional document itself and with the enactment of treason legislation by the first Congress.[4]

Kirchheimer observed that for governments, the prosecution of political crime may be a matter of necessity, of choice, or of convenience. Perhaps the most significant part of this statement is its assertion that the prosecution of politically motivated behavior may at times be necessary.[5] Recognition of this fact is essential. Although the necessity or near-necessity for political prosecution may arise in various situations, it is in cases of homicide and other acts of extreme violence that the urgency for clear and effective response becomes particularly insistent. In these cases the essential humanity of the victims of such acts must be seen to override all countervailing considerations.[6] Any government or society that is less than convinced of this proposition invites a time of troubles.[7] One of the most distressing social syndromes of the past decade, therefore, has been the apparent propensity of persons at both ends of the ideological spectrum to temporize in their condemnations of violence when the acts in question were understood as advancing or intended to advance their own political or social objectives.

The attitudes expressed toward the military conviction of Lieutenant William L. Calley are instructive in the respect. It would be difficult to doubt the conclusiveness of the evidence supporting the accused's guilt of multiple homicides.[8] Nevertheless, the public outcry against the conviction arose from both the right and left. The ground occupied by the right consists of an adamant refusal to believe that atrocities can be committed by anyone wearing an American uniform or, what amounts to the same thing, an insistence on the total immunity of American soldiers from punishment for acts committed in combat against the enemy or a foreign civilian population. From the other political extreme came an equally peremptory insistence that Lieutenant Calley must not be punished for murder, however guilty he might be of the acts charged against him, because colonels, generals, and other high political figures share that guilt and have not been held accountable. The importance of identifying all the culpable parties in such atrocities cannot reasonably be doubted; it is a very different matter, however, to permit suspicions of the complicity of others to provide immunity for the person immediately responsible for multiple killings. When politically motivated acts of extreme violence occur, a wise society does not confine itself to imposing penalties on the perpetrators but seeks in addition to locate the causes for such acts and, insofar as may be possible, to eliminate them. But a wise society does not recognize setoffs to murder.

Although they are necessary in some instances, prosecutions of political crimes, in this country and throughout the world, have often perpetrated injustices, exacerbated tensions and hostilities within societies, and incapacitated political communities from accurately perceiving reality or adapting rationally to it. Vital interests have thus been imperiled by prosecutions in these cases, and the interests endangered have been not only those of the accused in the criminal proceedings, but often those of the government that instituted the prosecution and of the larger society as well. The problems posed in this area are immeasurably complicated by the fact that simply to repeal all statutes proscribing politically motivated behavior is not a genuine option. This is true both because certain kinds of politically motivated behavior, such as acts of extreme violence, require resort to criminal sanctions by the government if its essential obligations are to be performed, and because such uses of the criminal process are believed to be necessary by the government and the larger part of the community. Thus, for a liberal society the problem of political crime, like most other issues that really matter, is a problem of more or less, of when and how. A series of difficult questions of both general and technical concern must be answered. How broadly should the net of criminal liability be spread when drafting penal legislation in this field? What sorts of surveillance and investigation are to be employed in ferreting out violations of the statutes? When should violations be disregarded, and when should vigorous prosecutorial efforts be made? Who among the many adhering to a political cause and eligible for prosecution should be named in the indictment? Should charges be limited to overt acts producing or threatening immediate harm or widely stated to include persons operating on the far periphery of conspiratorial action? What penalties should be imposed on the accused to express the community's sense of justice and to advance the long-term, as well as immediate, interests of the state? These and many more equally perplexing inquiries must be made; and how they are answered may substantially affect the security and well-being of a political society.

Inquiries of this sort, however, give rise to larger problems and perhaps larger doubts. In fact, the question arises whether useful general propositions can be made about political crime and the administration of law in this area. All of the familiar prudential strictures about the unreliability of untested and, in some cases, untestable generalizations assert themselves with unusual force. One reason lies in the extraordinary range of conduct that has been encompassed within the political offense concept, behavior extending from acts of protest that can best be described as forms of symbolic speech to assassinations and other sorts of violence that seriously endanger life and limb or inflict extensive injuries on property. Another souce of doubt resides in the difficulties of making even common-sense estimates of the actual social consequences that will result from the enactment of legislation proscribing particular kinds of politically motivated behavior or the bringing of a prosecution against the leaders of a political movement possessing significant popular support. The problems encountered in measuring the impact of enacting and administering legal sanctions are, of course, in no sense peculiar to the political crimes area. There is an almost total absence of systematic knowledge about the deterrent consequences of the criminal law and other sorts of regulatory sanctions, and until recently this ignorance has not caused substantial concern.[9] Even if these problems are in no sense unique to the political crime area, it is nevertheless true, as Johannes Andeneas suggested, that judgments about the consequences of political prosecutions require consideration, in part, of a range of factors distinctive to this field.[10]

Certainly the easy generalizations occasionally heard from persons of liberal disposition to the effect that political prosecutions ''do no good'' are entitled to be met with considerable skepticism. If such statements are meant to imply that well-publicized efforts to prevent and punish subversive activities of organized political movements in the past have often proved injurious to the long-term interests of American society, the proposition is entitled to sober consideration.[11] If, however, such statements are intended to cast doubt on the ability of governments sometimes to achieve their immediate political objectives through the device of political prosecution, the statement is dubious. Numerous instances can be cited in American history in which the government appears to have employed the criminal process to achieve specific repressive ends and to have succeeded in these objectives, however questionable the goals and whatever the effects of these endeavors on broader social values. The prosecution of the leaders of the International Workers of the World in the spring of 1918, and the subsequent criminal proceedings directed against the second-level leadership, appear to have effectively destroyed the influence of this organization as a political or economic force in American society. Not until the Christmas amnesty of President Franklin Roosevelt in 1933 were the last of the convicted I.W.W. leaders released from imprisonment.[12] The Palmer raids and the subsequent state prosecutions under criminal syndicalism, sedition, and red flag laws in the 1920s are believed by some to have drastically changed the character of the American radical movement and to have stripped the left-wing parties of overt popular support.[13] That these con-

52

sequences were the objectives of conscious governmental policy can hardly be doubted.

Recent American experience with political prosecutions is perhaps more ambiguous. Even so, it provides little support for the easy assumption that resort to criminal sanctions in these cases is inevitably self-defeating and incapable of achieving the government's immediate ends. It has been confidently asserted that the prosecution of Dr. Benjamin Spock and his codefendants for conspiracy to counsel selective service registrants to evade military service encouraged, rather than deterred, young people in their resistance to the draft and to the Vietnam War.[14] That the Spock prosecution and its aftermath represent something less than a glorious chapter in American legal history, and that in many cases it did indeed harden the resistance of the young to the war, are abundantly clear. Yet it also seems difficult to conclude with assurance that the demonstrated willingness of the government to protect the functioning of the military draft by instituting prosecutions against prominent public figures had no effect in deterring violations of the selective service law or that, in this respect, the ultimate consequence was clearly to produce more resistance to the law than compliance with it.

Estimating the effects of the Chicago Seven case raises somewhat different questions. That prosecution, the events preceding it, and its aftermath surely constitute one of the least attractive episodes in recent American history.[15] Viewed from the campus vantage point, the case clearly contributed to the polarization of American society in the closing years of the 1960s. Certainly it exacerbated the alienation of American young people. One may also reasonably suspect that it constituted a significant step toward the tragic consummation of events that occurred at Kent State University in the spring of 1970, but which might have occurred on almost any campus in the land. Although it is tempting to look back on the case as simply a record of futility and waste, unfortunately one cannot overlook the possibility that the prosecution, among all its deplorable consequences, may also have strengthened the political positions of some of those who initiated and supported it.

Of course, there can also be political prosecutions so ill-conceived and bizarre that the institution of criminal proceedings results in nothing but loss to the interests of the government, the accused, and the community. The federal prosecution brought in response to an alleged plot of Father Philip Berrigan and his codefendants to kidnap high government officials comes close to meriting this dubious distinction.[16] It is not easy to conceive what interests of the government were served by initiating these proceedings. It is even more difficult to identify the public values that were advanced in obtaining convictions, not for conspiracy, but for smuggling a letter out of a federal prison—an act not even defined as criminal under the provisions of a progressive correctional code like that recently enacted in the state of Illinois.[17] Nor does it seem likely that the public was edified by the spectacle or induced to experience a deeper sense of security by reason of the convictions.

The essence of the matter appears to be that in many instances the political prosecution is, or is seen to be, an avenue to achieve certain immediate political or governmental purposes, and that these possibilities provide powerful inducements for resort to criminal sanctions even when such action may threaten longer-term interests and values. It is this characteristic that renders the prosecution of political crimes particularly susceptible to unwise and even abusive use. In some instances, however, resort to criminal prosecutions or to administrative devices like deportation is strongly urged by vocal elements of the community, and these pressures may override the initial doubts and resistance of the officials who later initiate the action. For instance, in the months immediately preceding the infamous raids that bear his name, Attorney General A. Mitchell Palmer was castigated for his inaction in the face of an assumed radical menace. The Senate unanimously adopted a resolution calling upon the Attorney General "to advise and inform the Senate whether or not the Department of Justice had taken legal proceedings, and if not, why not, and if so to what extent, for the arrest and punishment . . . of the various persons within the United States who . . . have attempted to bring about the forcible overthrow of the

Government.'' Palmer himself, reflecting on the pressures to which he had been subjected, stated, probably with substantial accuracy: ''I say that I was shouted at from every editorial sanctum in America from sea to sea; I was preached upon from every pulpit; I was urged—I could feel it dinned into my ears—throughout the country to do something and do it now, and do it quick, and do it in a way that would bring results to stop this sort of thing in the United States.'' [18]

Despite the powerful inducements to the use of political prosecutions by governments, there may be powerful inhibitions as well. The same ambiguities that confront efforts to identify the consequences of such a proceeding after the fact confront even more seriously efforts to estimate the probable results before the proceeding is initiated. Even when the government is most concerned with immediate political gains and most unmindful of long-run consequences, the resort to criminal prosecution involves significant risks. Such a case requires the government to relinquish control of a situation and to place it in the hands of a judge and jury, who may be disposed to exercise their independence to the full. There is chanciness in the fact that the trial gives the accused a forum, and on more than one occasion the defense has demonstrated far greater skill in public communications than has the government. Public reactions may be unexpected. It is often unclear whether the public will be attentive to the proceedings or, should it become interested, whether its sympathies will lie with the hounds or the fox. These are the utilitarian considerations; there are other more fundamental uncertainties. Although unintended consequences inevitably accompany any social action, none of the ordinary functions of government is afflicted by greater ambiguities and uncertainties than is the prosecution of political offenders; and this is true whether one views these proceedings from the perspective of the government's interest or that of the larger society. Thus, if the problem of creating and administering a law of political crimes is a matter of more or less, of when and how, it is of particular importance to identify at least some of the factors that are productive of unintended consequences.

The consequences produced by prosecutions of political offenders are peculiarily dependent on the circumstances obtaining in society when the proceedings are held. Since such circumstances alter over time, one productive source of unintended consequences is miscalculations about the degree of social change that has occurred and about its nature. In looking back on American experiences earlier in the century, one is struck by the extent to which the dangerous alien was conceived of as the principal threat to internal security. In significant measure the frenetic resort to mass deportations, as well as to criminal sanctions, represented an expression of American nativism, with its suspicions and fears of strangers who appeared to threaten an entire life style that had come to be understood as distinctively American.[19] Perhaps a remnant of these attitudes can be seen in the strongly held belief of some middle western legislators in the 1960s that the student disorders on state university campuses were the product of admitting undesirables from the eastern seaboard into the student bodies. These beliefs, not being founded on fact, proved invulnerable to factual refutation. As in the case of aliens, the legislatures passed exclusion laws, which substantially limited the number of out-of-state students who might be admitted to the state universities. Although this legislation was primarily motivated by financial stringencies, the political factor was not insignificant, and sometimes was quite explicit.

There are significant differences between the recent past and earlier periods of anxiety about radical activity in this century, and one of the most important factors in producing these differences is the circumstance that in the late 1960s the groups producing concern—college students, racial and ethnic activists—were comprised overwhelmingly of native-born Americans. Although deportation has not lost all significance as a response to internal subversion, the concept of the dangerous alien played only a small part in the agitations of the last decade. This is a highly significant development, whose importance may not be fully appreciated, within or outside the government. Bumper stickers admonish one to love America or leave it; but those offering the warning have not suggested a means for compelling the latter alternative, unless prison or the concentration camp is seen to be the mode of exit.

An argument familiar to criminologists is that society "needs its criminals." The punishment of deviancy, it is suggested, represents a ritualistic reaffirmation of the community's values and strengthens the sense of personal worth of the noncriminal majority by identifying its members as parts of a group possessing distinctive convictions and aspirations.[20] This view might be thought to apply with particular force to the prosecution of political crimes. Thus, the punishment of the traitor both dramatizes the reality of the community and reinforces the sense of indentity of its constituent members. One need not deny all validity to these concepts to recognize that in a society in which consensus is suffering substantial erosion, the social effects of imposing punishment on political deviants may be quite different from that suggested by the theory. If the deviant is part of an infinitesimal minority, or a member of a large but powerless group, then his symbolic sacrifice to the values of the dominant group may conceivably enhance the vigor and cohesion of the majority. But if the deviant groups are substantial in size, assertive in demand, and vigorous in defense of their values, if they are recruited in significant measure from persons born close to the centers of power as well as from the dispossessed, attempts at criminal repression may produce a clamor that assaults the confidence of the majority group and which weakens rather than fortifies its sense of identity. To obtain the satisfying feeling of truth vindicated may then require a quantum of force not available to the majority or, if available and employed, which threatens or destroys the libertarian assumptions of the society. In short, the problems of administering the law of political crimes in the late 1960s proved to be significantly different from those that had been presented when the government pursued the specter of the dangerous alien; and one may suspect that the rather indifferent successes of recent political prosecutions reflect, in part, an incomplete awareness of these differences.

Not all the risks and social liabilities associated with the prosecution of political offenders, however, are to be explained by recent changes in the nature of political deviancy in the United States. On the contrary, the long history of such proceedings in various periods and cultures reveals a remarkable persistence of certain tendencies, many of which are often deleterious to general social interests and sometimes dangerous to the governments that frame and prosecute the criminal charges. Much of this history may be summarized in the proposition that the identification and punishment of political offenders tends strongly to excess. Excessive public reactions constitute one of its most significant forms. A repressive stance of the government may sometimes induce a popular supportive reaction exceeding anything the government contemplated or desires. This phenomenon was noted by the younger Pliny when, as a provincial Roman governor, he sought advice from Emperor Trajan on how to adminster sanctions against those who professed Christianity. "Now as I have begun to deal with this problem, as so often happens," he wrote, "the charges are becoming more widespread and increasing in variety. An anonymous pamphlet has been circulated which contains the names of a number of accused persons." Trajan replied, counseling moderation in the procedures to be employed, and to his enduring credit added: "But pamphlets circulated anonymously must play no part in any accusations. They create the worst sort of precedent and are quite out of keeping with the spirit of our age." [21] Unfortunately, wisdom like Trajan's rarely enlightens the governance of any society.

The tendency to excess is seen also in judicial behavior. Although full recognition should be given to the numerous honorable exceptions, it is nevertheless remarkable how often in widely separated historical periods the overreaching and arbitrary behavior of judges appears to have been associated with the prosecution of political offenders. The judge "conducted the trial with malicious ferocity . . . [E]very ruling throughout the long trial on any contested point was in favor of the State and . . . page after page of the record contained insinuating remarks of the judge . . . with the evident intent of bringing the jury to his way of thinking." [22] These words do not refer to a recent event but were spoken by Governor Peter Altgeld of Illinois in

1893 about the performance of the trial judge in the Haymarket case. Commenting on the political trials of the Roman Empire, Montesquieu observed, "Tiberius always found judges ready to condemn as many people as he could suspect." [23] In late eighteenth-century England the series of prosecutions for criminal libel and sedition in which Thomas Erskine gained his reputation as a defender of liberty were characterized by judicial extravagance. "God help the people who have such judges," said Charles James Fox.[24]

Judicial excess is often reflected in the imposition of excessive sentences. It is here that governments often lose the verdict of history. Now, long after the events, one may doubt that the interests of the British people were well served by the imposition of the death penalty on Roger Casement or that the United States was advantaged by the capital sentences in the *Rosenberg* case.[25] Memories of such incidents have long lives and are often carefully cultivated by the political minorities from which the convicted offenders arose; and after time has passed, the steady attrition of the minority often convinces the majority that a serious injustice has been done. More broadly, it can be said that policies of political repression, however enthusiastically supported when devised, tend in the long run to damage the reputation of governments and to fare poorly at the hands of history.[26] Perhaps the reason is that those who make history do not ordinarily write it. In any event, even the fearsome Wobbly who invaded the dreams of our fathers and grandfathers tends now to be recalled as a quaint and lovable folk hero who produced a book of first-rate songs.

These and other evidences of excess are symptomatic of the unique stresses that prosecutions of political crimes create in the institutions of justice. In large measure these stresses arise from the basic fact on which the political offense concept rests, namely, that persons who commit political crimes are ordinarily different in significant respects from other criminals. Studies of the attitudes and beliefs of common criminals reveal that such persons tend to accept the conventional values of the community, including the values embodied in the criminal law that they have been charged with violating. To be sure, offenders are adept at discovering reasons to excuse their own behavior or to "neutralize" official values when applied to their own situations.[27] It probably remains true, however, that most prisoners do not challenge the broad principles of the criminal law, nor do they reject the legitimacy of the government institutions that administer it, however quick they may be to charge mistaken or abusive uses of state power in their own cases. Moreover, to a remarkable degree the procedures of criminal justice depend on and receive the cooperation of the accused and his counsel, even in cases in which conviction of the defendant is all but inevitable and the penalties to be imposed are serious. As the David M. Potter observed: "The unanimity with which in the past, accused persons accepted this system was so total that we were not even aware of the naked vulnerability of the courts until the Chicago Seven disclosed it to us." [28]

The "political" defendant creates very different burdens and tensions for the institutions of justice. He often seeks to test the values and motives of the official agencies against his own and thereby to subject justice to trial. His efforts in this connection may be carefully deliberated. "In court," wrote Father Philip Berrigan, "one puts values against legality according to legal rules and with slight chance of legal success. One does not look for justice; one hopes for a forum from which to communicate ideals, convictions, and anguish." And again: "When it comes to defending political dissenters like ourselves, lawyers become accomplices in the game against us—if, that is, they play its rules." [29] The defendant obtains sustenance for his resolve in the conviction that his own values and purposes have received a higher validation than can be conferred by the legal order, and in the belief that his efforts and sacrifices may advance the welfare and happiness of human beings. He may be sustained also by the fact that in some sense he is not alone. Characteristically, political crimes grow out of group activity, the size of the group and the effectiveness of its organization varying, of course, from case to case.[30] Even when the defendant finds himself defeated in his efforts to express and advance his political values in the courtroom, his associates and supporters outside the courthouse will often subject the proceedings to a drumfire of criticism and protest. The prosecution of a political offender may therefore involve two trials: the one in which the accused must respond to the charges brought against him by the government, and the other in which the court and the agencies of government are subjected to a kind of prosecution in the community. One substantial risk for the government is that, although it may win in the courtroom, it may lose in the larger tribunal.[31]

The German historian Theodore Mommsen once observed: "Impartiality in political trials is about on the level with the Immaculate Conception: one may wish for it but one cannot produce it." [32] The remark would possess greater pertinence if it had been addressed less to the fact of partiality than to the appearance of unfairness. The history of political prosecutions affords innumerable instances of biased and corrupted tribunals from which justice and equity were excluded. A society determined to do so, however, can presumably minimize problems of this sort; but in political cases the task of protecting the good reputation of courts for justice and impartiality, even when unusual efforts are made to achieve fairness, may prove insuperable. The difficulties of creating, not only the reality, but the appearance of justice for all interested segments of the community can result in serious losses of confidence for the system of criminal justice. These difficulties may arise from many causes, but the essential problem is the absence of underlying premises and propositions held in common by the tribunal and the defense.[33] This lack of common assumptions produces widely differing perceptions of what is relevant to the criminal proceedings. A sense of the impartiality of the court and the fairness of the proceedings is difficult to maintain in the accused and his supporters when the tribunal's standards of relevance exclude from the trial consideration of the very matters that have motivated the defendant's behavior and for which he has spent his energies and hazarded his freedom. That the judge's criteria are correct or are even the only possible legal basis on which the trial can proceed does not soften the sense of injustice felt by the defendant and by the groups who identify with his cause.[34]

The threat of political prosecutions to the reputation of courts for justice and equity was aggravated by certain events that culminated in the political trials of the late 1960s. For good or ill the courts, in facing the crises of the time, asserted judicial powers with great boldness. *Brown* v. *School Board* was the precipitating cause of much of the activity, but a great deal of it was carried on in areas other than those involving race relations.[35] The period, therefore, was not one to emphasize the limits of judicial power or to encourage recognition of the fact that the accommodation of judicial authority to the institutions of majority rule remains one of the fundamental problems of the American system. A whole generation of young people, as well as of social scientists, grew to maturity uninstructed in the inhibitions on judicial power. As a result, many young persons were wholly unprepared for the reluctance of the courts to confront such extraordinary political questions as the legality of the Vietnam War or, in trials of war resisters, to immunize individual conscience from the reach of state power. Surprise grew into anger and disillusionment; and the courts, which had formerly been the chief reliance of these groups to achieve rapid and fundamental social reforms, were now denounced as tools and instrumentalities of the political establishment. In the meantime, ironically, there were reactions from the other end of the political spectrum designed to limit the free exercise of judicial powers in sensitive political areas, as exemplified by the enactment of the Omnibus Crime Bill of 1968 and the proposals for legislative and even constitutional change engendered by the busing controversy.[36] The exercise of judicial power, of course, cannot and ought not to be divorced from the political life of the nation. Certain sorts of involvement, however, not only threaten the reputation of courts for equity and impartiality but may also weaken the capacity of the courts to retain their powers intact.

Administration of the law of political crimes has provided other sources of stress for the institutions of criminal justice. One of the most important involves the problems associated with the exercise of prosecutorial discretion. Prosecutions of political crimes, while relatively numerous in recent years, have resulted in few impressive successes for the government; and in several instances such victories as were achieved in the trial courts vanished on appeal. Illustrative are the loss of the conspiracy counts in the trial of the Chicago Seven case and the reversal of all the convictions on appeal, the reversal in the Spock case and the direction of acquittal for two of the defendants by the appellate court, the acquittal of black militants Angela Davis and Bobby Seale, and the curious result in the Berrigan prosecution at Harrisburg.[37] These prosecutorial misadventures may not have been entirely unproductive of social advantage. At the least, the very meagerness of success in these cases serves to refute the more extreme libels of American criminal justice that have been voiced both at home and overseas, and surely demonstrates that these trials were genuine contests, not choreographed rituals of the sort sometimes produced in totalitarian states.

The satisfactions to be derived from this record, however, must be measured. For the failure of a prosecution is likely to raise the question posed by Angela Davis immediately upon her acquittal: Why was this prosecution brought at all? [38] The question, of course, smacks of wisdom after the event, and in many instances the suspicion it articulates is wholly unfounded. It is not always possible before the trial to estimate accurately the strength of the prosecutor's case. Moreover, as the recently formulated Standards of Criminal Justice recognize, there may be situations in which a prosecutor is under obligation to institute criminal proceedings even when a favorable jury response is in doubt.[39] Nevertheless, recent history has raised substantial questions about the exercise of the prosecutor's discretion, and one suspects that some of these problems have a special affinity for the political crimes area.

There is evidence that the unfettered exercise of the prosecutor's discretion to determine against whom criminal proceedings are to be instituted and the largely uncontrolled determination of the scope and nature of the criminal charge are evoking increasing restiveness in the United States. The basic complaints are not only that the powers are largely unsupervised and, when unwisely or vindictively employed, capable of inflicting great harm on the persons accused, but also that even when properly exercised, the decisions are rarely explained or publicly justified. These issues are by no means confined to the prosecution of political offenders, but as is true of other problems, they tend to be magnified and to take on more serious aspects when political crimes are involved.

Something of the distinctive character of the problem of prosecutorial discretion in cases of political crimes is suggested by the comments of two highly qualified observers. In 1940, then Attorney General Robert H. Jackson wrote: ''In times of fear or hysteria political, racial, religious, social and economic groups, often from the best of motives, cry for the scalps of individuals or groups because they do not like their views. Particularly do we need to be dispassionate and courageous in those cases which deal with so-called 'subversive activities.' They are dangerous to civil liberty because the prosecutor has no definite standards to determine what constitutes a 'subversive activity,' such as we have for murder or larceny.'' And in the nineteenth century Henry Cockburn, reflecting on the British state trials for sedition, remarked: ''The only way to prevent . . . sympathy with crime is to be sure that it is guilt and for its own sake that it is prosecuted and that it is properly tried. And it is not enough that guilt be real. It ought also to be great. Even a conviction for a weak case does no good.'' [40]

These comments suggest that in political cases the proper exercise of the prosecutor's discretion places unusual demands on the wisdom and fortitude of public officials. That these requirements are not always fully satisfied is not surprising. The very absence of articulated grounds for the exercise of prosecutorial discretion creates unusual hazards of uninformed and unwarranted criticism. The conclusion is nevertheless unavoidable that in some of the highly publicized cases of recent years dubious decisions were made. Would the indictment in the Harrisburg-Berrigan case have been returned, or returned in the particular form that it took, had not the Department of Justice felt constrained to vindicate the sensational charges made publicly before a congressional committee by the Director of the Federal Bureau of Investigation? What of the suspicious symmetry in the indictments returned following the disorders at the 1968 Democratic Convention in Chicago: one indictment charging eight policemen with violating the civil rights act, the other charging eight demonstrators under the federal antiriot law? [41] Did the government adequately anticipate the tensions and skepticism engendered by its decision to prosecute the Spock case under a broad conspiracy theory when narrower and perhaps more credible grounds were presumably available? [42] And how were the particular defendants selected for inclusion in the indictment out of the large number of persons who appeared to be equally eligible? [43] Selection of the defendants in the Spock case is reminiscent of a comment attributed to Brainerd Currie when paying a visit to a faculty colleague's apartment, located in one of the more venerable and decrepit buildings on Chicago's South Side. The living room ceiling was crisscrossed by cracks, and in several places the plaster had entirely given way. When the host pointed with pride to an area of the ceiling that had recently been repaired by the landlord, Currie gave the repairs a searching glance and, after due deliberation, asked, "How did the landlord know *that* was the spot to repair?"

Prosecutors' decisions that appear to be erroneous or dubious, however, may be manifestations of genuine dilemmas for those performing these functions. Edmund Burke confessed that he did not know how to indict a whole people, and it may be similarly difficult to indict a popular political movement with an active membership numbering in the tens of thousands. Any selection of defendants for an exemplary prosecution in such a case is likely to create the appearance of arbitrariness and inequity, an impression that the political opposition will be quick to exploit. Problems of this sort arise, of course, in the prosecution of ordinary crimes. The deterrent theory of criminal punishment, which may result in severe penalties being imposed on an accused principally to induce other persons to comply with the law, creates substantial moral problems for some critics.[44] But rarely in the administration of the law of ordinary crimes is the prosecutor confronted by so many persons equally guilty and accessible for prosecution as in some political cases. The problem is not eased by the consideration that the political opposition may deliberately attempt to goad the prosecution into initiating more proceedings than the system can tolerate and thus, by surcharging the agencies of justice, bring them to a halt.[45]

Dilemmas are also confronted when one seeks means to render the exercise of the prosecutor's discretion more responsible. Except in unusual circumstances, public opinion does not constitute an effective limitation. These decisions are ordinarily of low visibility, and the public is likely to be uninformed and not vitally interested. In such circumstances, if the question is considered at all, the public will indulge a "presumption of regularity." Even when public disapproval is a fact, it will rarely threaten the over-all popular support of a political regime. A national administration successful at the polls may thus be slow to credit and respond to whatever popular disapproval exists.

Extraordinarily abusive exercises of the prosecutor's discretion may sometimes be curbed by judicial intervention.[46] There are genuine problems, however, associated with court supervision of prosecutorial decisions. The most important is the danger of confusing salutary with improper uses of discretion. It does not follow that past decisions to avoid prosecution should invariably bar subsequent prosecutions in apparently similar situations. It may sometimes be the better part of wisdom for the prosecutor to ignore political demonstrations, for example, even when technically illegal acts have been committed. There may be a realistic hope that a mild reaction will discourage future violations, or a defensible judgment that the consequences of prosecution may prove more serious than the acts perpetrated by the demonstrators. Events may prove such judgments to have been in error, and the time may come when the decision is reached that the unlawfulness can no longer be tolerated and that criminal proceedings are now required. Surely such a judgment should be permitted. Indeed, if the prosecutor, by withholding prosecution, runs the risk of impotence when action is required, the consequence may be to encourage the initiation of proceedings in cases that might more wisely be ignored, in order to preserve his future position.

66

Nevertheless, the need for greater responsibility in the exercise of prosecutorial discretion is real, and nowhere is this more evident than in the prosecution of political crimes. Substantial sharing of these decisions is sometimes required to ensure that a broader consideration of the interests and impacts will be given than is likely to be contributed by the prosecutor himself or by his immediate bureaucratic superiors.[47] A public statement of prosecutorial policy is required, as is machinery designed to render decision making visible and the decision makers accountable.[48] The needs are clear, but even the most sanguine should not assume that appropriate institutional accommodation will be made or that, if devised, the machinery will prove adequate to the needs. Administration of the law of political crimes is characterized by an essential unruliness. This is perhaps its most striking and enduring feature. Success here is to be measured, not by the ability to solve problems or to eliminate difficulties, but by the capacity to contain the losses within tolerable margins.

One of the problems encountered in administering any system of sanctions, which is particularly acute in efforts to control politically motivated behavior, is the need to retain a realistic view of the broad purposes intended to be served. The object of survival is not necessarily the most ignoble purpose of government. In any case, it is an inevitable one. Yet frequently governmental policy in this area weakens rather than strengthens the stability of regimes, as has been shown in both the modern era and the past. So frequently has this occurred, as in the period of the nineteenth century following the Congress of Vienna, that one is tempted to conclude that launching a program of counterrevolutionary repression is among the most hazardous courses a government can pursue.

It should be recognized, first, that systems of criminal justice display the weaknesses that generally typify bureaucratic specialization. The measures proposed and applied—whether preventive detention, registration of political agents, electronic eavesdropping, deportation, or arrest and imprisonment—become ends in themselves, often pursued with an enthusiasm bordering on fanaticism and rarely subjected to the test of whether they actually advance the purposes that presumably motivated their adoption in the first instance. The ordinary bureaucratic tendencies are enhanced by the character and temperament of some of the persons who apply government policy in the political crimes area. The fanaticism of the terrorist is sometimes matched by the fanaticism of the government agent. A kind of religious warfare results, with neither side revealing any disposition to doubt the virtue of its cause or to subject the efficacy of its means and measures to critical examination. The Watergate incident provided a glimpse of this fanaticism and its implications. If there is anything more deplorable than the acts committed in that and related incidents, it is the reasons publicly stated to explain and justify them.[49] Although fanaticism of this sort may sometimes produce shrewdness and daring, it is more likely to breed unrealism, indeed stupidity, in adapting a particular policy or program to the structure of overarching values it is intended to strengthen and support. Although American society shows many instances of specialization gone mad, some of the most striking and dangerous examples are found in the secret police and intelligence agencies.

The United States has left to the police and prosecuting agencies, without even the assistance of meaningful, publicly stated standards of performance, the intricate task of adapting programs of law enforcement to the attainment of larger political values. To report that these agencies have proved inadequate to the task is to condemn not them but the community. The problem is made more acute by the fact that some of these agencies have achieved remarkably untrammeled volition to determine not only what they will do but also what and how much the public is entitled to learn about their activities. These circumstances breed a kind of bureaucratic obtuseness, which in times of stress can be dangerous, for it confuses public reactions and may deny support for the government in cases where it is deserved. The task of frustrating the activities of political terrorists, for example, is surely a legitimate function of government. But this task should not include the harrassment of groups organized to advance political objectives through constitutionally protected means, however unpopular or even unwise those objectives may be. That the nation's secret police, both state and federal, have stooped to such harrassment has often been alleged, and the evidence supporting these allegations has not always been convincingly refuted.[50] Yet nothing is more calculated to breed and sustain political extremism than is the widely held and apparently supported belief that in the political arena American police are regularly, sometimes deliberately, flouting the principles on which the country's polity is based.

The task of identifying and controlling the political terrorist is one of extraordinary difficulty, chiefly because political crime is involved. It is apparent that a police agency can not proceed to identify persons who have engaged in acts of political violence, like the planting of time bombs in bank vaults, without placing under surveillance a great deal of noncriminal political activity and large numbers of persons who have not and never will descend to acts of violence and terror. Thus, the police function in these cases is in constant danger of impinging on the basic political values of the community. It is an alarming circumstance that in large segments of American society, even legitimate and vitally necessary police activity is conceived of as oppressive. This is true in part because the police have on occasion violated political values or revealed insensitivity to and even ignorance of these values, and accordingly have made both themselves and the political compact vulnerable to corrosive suspicion. The danger, however, is not only that the police may be denied support when it is deserved, but also that in other segments of the community the police may gain support when it is undeserved. Police practices that regularly disregard basic restraints may teach the community that security can be achieved in no other way. If believed, the lesson strips one of the capacity for indignation when political values are invaded by official authority. Without that capacity, those values cannot survive.

Administration of the law of political crimes is often a necessary, and surely an inevitable, government function. Yet all experience with the political prosecution supports the prediction that in the future, as in the past, such proceedings will sometimes be launched that are neither necessary nor wise. So long as governments can obtain immediate political gains from the trial of a political case, decisions will occasionally be made to proceed with prosecutions injurious to the long-term interests of the community. This is true, not only because the prospects of immediate gain are often a more powerful determinant of behavior than are fears of a speculative future loss, but also because the undesirable consequences are often unexpected and unforeseen, and therefore do not serve as effective deterrents of unwise behavior.

Justification for a quiescent fatalism must not be derived from this situation. The American public has today acquired a much broader experience with these problems than was possessed in the days of the red scare at the end of the First World War or even in the era of Senator Joseph McCarthy in the 1950s. The unintended consequences of efforts to control politically motivated behavior need not prove so surprising and unpredictable in the future as in the past. Certain propositions about public policy in the area can now be stated with reasonable confidence. For instance, the experience of the last generation offers little to recommend a repetition of mass political trials of the sort represented by the Chicago Seven case or by the prosecution of native Fascists and proto-Fascists in the Second World War.[51] Such proceedings have rarely contributed to national security, and they have often eroded support for the institutions of justice. A growing skepticism about the uses of the conspiracy device, especially in cases impinging on First Amendment rights, strongly counsels an increased emphasis on the demonstrable overt act as a basis for criminal prosecutions in this area.[52] Discretion will always play an essential role in the administration of criminal justice, including that relating to the law of political crimes. But there is a pressing need to guarantee greater responsibility in the exercise of discretion by prosecutors and by police agencies performing surveillance functions. Explicit statements of policy outlining areas of jurisdiction, techniques to be employed, and procedures to be pursued are required; and ma-

70

chinery adequate to supervise decision making and to hold public officials accountable who abuse their authority should be devised.[53] Realization of such measures will of course require intelligence and will, as does any public effort to affect and strengthen policy.

Among the most important issues raised by the law of political crimes and its administration is the relation of the political crime concept to the perfromance of the criminal justice function in cases of ordinary criminality. The area of political crimes is only one part, and rarely the most important part, of the administration of criminal justice. The influence of ideas and practices given birth in the prosecution of political offenders on the criminal law in general, therefore, becomes a matter of importance and justifiable concern.

Modern experience suggests that attitudes and procedures devised in the political crimes area, including those that are most dangerous and dubious, are not and cannot be confined to the political prosecution. On the contrary, there is a strong tendency for these practices to infect and characterize the performance of the justice function in all areas. Recent events have demonstrated the difficulties of compartmentalizing pratices and policies in any single area of concern. Thus, surveillance practices first employed by the government in conducting the cold war of international politics were later used to combat domestic radicalism and even to gain mere partisan political advantage. The same practices may be expected to characterize government activity in the area of orgainzed crime. This propensity for expansion, accompanied as it is by the rise of computer and electronic technology, thus threatens the integrity of the justice function on which the liberties and securities of ordinary individuals depend.[54]

American experience with the political crime concept has other points of relevance for one pondering the more general problems of criminal justice. Indeed, this experience throws light on the nature and limitations of the criminal sanction as a device for the achievement of policy objectives. The political crimes area is not only afflicted by the problems associated with administering any system of coercive sanctions, but also encompasses special risks and social liabilities. Many of the risks are associated with the fact that every political trial contains the potential of an assault on the legitimacy of the law and the institutions of justice by the accused and his organized supporters in the community. A strong constitutional regime will ordinarily survive these assaults, but no system of justice thrives when its basic authority is continually placed in question.

A pervasive weakness of the administration of justice in the political crimes area is therefore its tendency to produce offenders supported by organized groups who challenge the law and the regime that administers it on grounds of principle. The political offender seeks to advance not only his personal interests but also a principle, and his principles are in some measure antagonistic to those expressed by the agencies of justice. Such a confrontation may not always produce insuperable difficulties for a government, but the resistance encountered by official agencies ordinarily limits the effectiveness of the criminal sanction and enhances the social costs of criminal prosecutions. It is important to recognize, however, that the ''political'' ingredient in the political crimes concept is a volatile, not a stable, element; and given appropriate conditions, whole areas of the criminal law that were formerly conceived of as involving common crimes against persons and property can quickly be transformed into areas of political crime. In situations of extreme political disruption the entire criminal justice function may be seen as political; and when this happens, the vital contributions to public order that the criminal law is expected to provide may no longer be available.

In order to avoid the difficulties and disabilities associated with the prosecution and prevention of political crimes, it therefore becomes a matter of first importance in the administration of criminal justice to discourage, so far as possible, the perception of acts of ordinary criminality as political crimes. Yet decisions by the legislatures to make certain behavior criminal, or by the police and the courts to use certain methods, may result in the creation of what are essentially new areas of political offenses, accompanied by all the difficulties and costs associated with the administration of justice when political crimes are involved. For example, one fundamental explanation of popular attitudes that deprive the system of criminal justice of the support of increasingly large groups within American society is the very breadth of attempted criminal regulation. Many years ago a veteran student of the police function made the point that the automobile had done much to deprive the police of the spontaneous support of the community.[55] Because many traffic violations are criminal, and because most adults are drivers, a majority of adults for the first time became potential criminals. The interests of the population, therefore, have become in some measure adverse to the system of law enforcement. This opposition is strengthened by the fact that even innocent acts of the driver may be classified as criminal or quasicriminal, as well as that traffic regulations are often applied in an abrasive way.

Far more serious are the factors that have encouraged the separation of young people from the institutions of adult society. The conscious dynamics of the youth culture and probably even more so its unconscious motivations operate to create differences that distinguish it from adult society. These differences, including the use of marijuana, have involved inhabitants of the youth culture in hostile confrontations with the police and the other apparatus of the criminal law. There has developed in some young people a flaming conviction that the system of criminal justice is inhumanely repressive and threatening to personal integrity and volition. These attitudes, gained in many cases from first-hand experience or observation, may take on significant political dimensions, for they create a numerous constituency responsive to political movements predicated on the assumption of the injustice and oppression of existing social institutions. It is likely that in this area of drugs the penal policy is exacting costs that cannot be prudently sustained.

Prediction is hazardous, but indications of the last decade suggest a future characterized by a greater degree of self-conciousness and assertiveness on the part of groups defined by age, ethnic background, religious commitment, and perhaps in other

73

ways as well. It seems probable that if something like the free society is to be achieved in the years ahead, it will be the product of a broader tolerance of diversity in interpersonal relations, ethical imperatives, and private conduct. The notion of the melting pot is today antagonistic to political and personal freedom, for it could only be achieved through massive governmental coercion or a tide of repressive social conformity. These considerations are of the highest importance to the criminal law, for the tolerance on which rest our hopes for the only species of liberal society likely to be available in the future must be reflected first and foremost in the criminal law and its administration. This is the true significance of the decriminalization movement in the area of sumptuary regulation.[56] The continued effort to impose an official version of propriety in this area will probably fail, and at great cost. But the costs of success would likely be higher, for success could be achieved only through a kind of counterrevolutionary effort leading to a society as repressive as the hyperboles of radical reform assert it to be already.

Ordinary crimes against persons and property—behavior that by any test falls within the proper concern of the law—may also be converted into something very like political crimes by the methods employed in law enforcement. For many years this society has experienced frustration because of its apparent inability to cope successfully with serious criminality. One of the consequences has been the rise of what might be called the "war theory" of law enforcement. As long ago as 1937, Max Radin observed:

We are invited periodically, in the newspapers, from the pulpit, on the air, to engage in a war on crime. The military metaphor is so persistent and carried out in such detail, that we can scarcely help taking it for granted that somewhere before us, there is an intrenched and hostile force consisting of men we call criminals, whose purpose it is to attack Society, that is to say, us. The matter is presented as a simple enough affair, and it is assumed that if we fight valiantly, we shall win and conquer the enemy.

And then? Unfortunately, we are not quite clear what is to happen then.[57]

Wars are attended by certain inconveniences, one of which is a war psychology that, with only slight encouragement from circumstances or special pleading, can be quickly converted into a war psychosis. A society in such a mental state is not likely to achieve an accurate grasp of reality, to establish sensible priorities, or to make correct calculations of the social costs involved in policy alternatives. Evidence of these distorted perceptions abounds in contemporary statements about law enforcement. Thus, one frequently encounters the reflex in politicians and law enforcement spokesmen that attributes disturbing criminal occurrences to nationwide conspiracies, usually of a radical cast, or to the efforts of "outside agitators." Few of these assertions are ever confirmed by competent evidence. The events surrounding the Attica affair provide frightening illustrations of such misapprehensions of reality and their consequences. In a story dated September 14, 1971, and distributed widely through the national media, an assistant state correction commissioner was quoted as saying: "We have eyewitnesses who saw the hostages' throats cut—and we believe their reports." The autopsy evidence of the next day establishing that no throats were cut and that the victims died of gunshot wounds inflicted by the assaulting forces is startling enough.[58] What is still more revealing and suggestive, however, are the reactions of disbelief of the medical evidence displayed by many of those involved and by the public at large. Conceptions of who the "enemy" is and of his nature, when erroneous, can prepare the path to disaster.

The war theory of law enforcement has induced police departments in several urban communities to embark on programs of "aggressive patrol," which have led officers to enter high crime areas of central cities in disguise. These tactics have brought on sharp and violent contacts with dangerous criminals. Some of these persons are apprehended or killed. As the pattern unfolds, however, police officers are injured or die; and police forces, in vindictive retaliation, seek out the offenders, invade the privacy of persons in their homes, engage in unlawful detention of suspects, violate the rights and assault the dignity of those supposedly advantaged by such programs of law enforcement.[59] The inhabitants of these neighborhoods, sorely oppressed already by private criminality, leave no doubt that at such times it is the activities of the police that are more to be feared and resented. What is perhaps most ironic about these occurrences is that there is no convincing evidence that they contribute to the over-all effectiveness of law enforcement, and there is considerable reason to suspect that they produce the contrary result. Albert Reiss pointed out that by far the larger part of arrests, and hence of convictions, are initiated by citizen complaints to the police.[60] It follows that programs which alienate the citizenry from the police and which, among other things, inhibit citizen cooperation in law enforcement will, in the long run, reduce the effectiveness of the police function. Whether these and other results follow from policies of "aggressive patrol" is surely a researchable question.[61] But the war theory of law enforcement, by focusing on the elimination of criminals in particular cases, rarely leads the police to pose such questions.

The issue goes beyond the matter of law enforcement efficiency. One who elects to launch a war on crime should be aware that he is electing to engage in civil war. The concept is one that a liberal society cannot afford to harbor. The security of life and possessions from criminal interference is one of the blessings of liberty and domestic tranquillity that American constitutional arrangements are committed to advance. The criminal law has important contributions to make to the securing of these ends. But the devastating and stigmatic penalties of the criminal law are compatible with the spirit of a liberal society only when there is consensus about the necessity for penalizing the conduct defined as criminal and about the means employed in applying the law. Extension of the criminal law beyond these limits not only results in indifferent success in the areas to which the law is extended, but may also threaten its effectiveness in traditional applications. Beyond these limits lies the area of most political crimes.

A first principle of statesmanship in the formulation of penal policy should therefore be to confine the area of political crime to its narrowest possible limits. This goal entails fidelity to the proposition that the scope of political crimes must not be inadvertently expanded through dubious decisions to criminalize behavior of doubtful detriment to society or through the reckless

76

use of law enforcement measures that produce outrage in the community and principled opposition to the agencies of justice. Even within the traditional confines of the political crimes concept a wise restraint is required. ''There must be power,'' wrote Bertrand Russell, ''either that of governments, or that of anarchic adventurers. There must even be naked power so long as there are rebels against govenments, or even ordinary criminals. But if human life is to be, for the mass of mankind, anything better than a dull misery punctuated with moments of sharp horror, there must be as little naked power as possible.'' [62] So long as the political behavior of individuals and groups threatens the interests and values that the majority is entitled to defend, statutes defining political crimes will be drafted and political prosecutions initiated. But this activity is likely to entail high social costs and must be justified by the principle of strict necessity; and when the necessity is ended, the criminal law should promptly withdraw and attend to its routine but indispensable tasks.

Notes   Index

Notes

1. OF SCHOLARS, CRIME, AND POLITICS

1. Aristotle, *Politics* 1. 1253a.
2. A. M. Schlesinger, Jr., *The Politics of Upheaval,* vol. 3: *The Age of Roosevelt* (Boston: Houghton, Mifflin, 1960); *The Politics of Education* (London, 1886); Arend Lijphart, *The Politics of Accommodation* (Berkeley: University of California Press, 1968); S. J. Makeilski, *The Politics of Zoning* (New York: Columbia University Press, 1966); Myron Weiner, *The Politics of Scarcity* (Chicago: University of Chicago Press, 1962); J. P. Young, *The Politics of Affluence* (Chicago: Science Research Associates, 1968); M. R. Marrus, *The Politics of Assimilation* (Oxford: Clarendon Press, 1971); O. M. Lynch, *The Politics of Untouchability* (New York: Columbia University Press, 1969); Melvin Richter, *The Politics of Conscience* (Cambridge: Harvard University Press, 1964); D. A. Rustow, *The Politics of Compromise* (Princeton: Princeton University Press, 1955); A. M. Schlesinger, Jr., *The Politics of Hope* (London: Eyre and Spottswoode, 1964); Hadley Cantril, *The Politics of Despair* (New York: Collier Books, 1962); E. T. Jorsted, *The Politics of Doomsday* (Nashville: Abingdon Press, 1970); T. F. Leary, *The Politics of Ecstacy* (New York: Putnam, 1968); E. O. Stillman, *The Politics of Hysteria* (New York: Harper and Row, 1964); H. E. Read, *The Politics of the Unpolitical* (London: Routledge, 1943); R. D. Laing, *The Politics of Experience* (New York: Pantheon Books, 1967); Edwin Muir, *The Politics of King Lear* (Jackson: Glasgow, 1947); E. S. Ions, *The Politics of John F. Kennedy* (London: Routledge, 1967); Robert Meredith, *The Politics of the Universe* (Nashville: Vanderbilt University Press, 1968); H. J. Schonfield, *The Politics of God* (London: Hutchinson, 1970).
3. Sonia Orwell and Ian Angus, eds., *The Collected Essays, Journalism and Letters of George Orwell* (London: Secker and Warburg, 1968), IV, 408–409.

4. Albert Camus, *Resistance, Rebellion, and Death* (New York: Modern Library, 1963), p. 190.

5. R. L. Beals, *Politics of Social Research* (Chicago: Aldine, 1969), pp. 1, v.

6. E. M. Forster, *Two Cheers for Democracy* (New York: Harcourt, Brace, and World, 1951), p. 43.

7. See Yale Kamisar, *When the Cops Were Not "Handcuffed"* in D. R. Cressey, ed., *Crime and Criminal Justice* (Chicago: Quadrangle Press, 1971), pp. 46–57. See also T. F. T. Plucknett, *Edward I and Criminal Law* (Cambridge: Cambridge University Press, 1960), p. 29: "It will be enough if we bear in mind that our concerns with the enforcement of criminal law will compel us to remember that some great matters are involved, and that the whole fabric of government may be at issue when we discuss criminal procedure. Indeed, much of the domestic policy of kings such as Cnut and Edward the Confessor turned upon their attitudes to the persistent problem of the criminal, and most of what we know about their local institutions is, in fact, concerned with their activities in the ancient but perennial task of catching thieves; if we try to picture them as deliberating on policy or levying rates, we shall gravely misinterpret them and mistake their place in the framework of government."

8. R. G. Caldwell, *Criminology* (New York: Ronald Press, 1956); M. B. Clinard, *Sociology of Deviant Behavior* (New York: Rinehart, 1957), pp. 157–158, 169–170, 247–249; E. H. Sutherland, *Principles of Criminology,* 4th ed. (New York: Lippincott, 1947), pp. 179–184, 244–246, 280–284, 431; D. R. Taft, *Criminology: A Cultural Interpretation,* rev. ed. (New York: Macmillan, 1950), p. 342. For a more explicitly political view, see G. B. Vold, *Theoretical Criminology* (New York: Oxford University Press, 1958).

9. On the rehabilitative ideal, see F. A. Allen, *The Borderland of Criminal Justice: Essays in Law and Criminology* (Chicago: University of Chicago Press, 1964), pp. 24–41.

10. "I foresee the day when we could convert the worst criminal into a decent, respectable citizen in a matter of a few months—or perhaps even less time than that. The danger is, of course, that we could also do the opposite: we could change any decent, respectable citizen into a criminal . . . We should reshape our society so that we all would be trained from birth to want what society wants us to do. We have the techniques now to do it." J. V. McConnell, "Criminals Can Be Brainwashed—Now," *Psychology Today,* April 1970, pp. 74–75, quoted in S. L. Halleck, *The Politics of Therapy* (New York: Science House, 1971). See also Anthony Burgess, *The Clockwork Orange* (New York: Norton, 1963).

11. See Francis A. Allen, "Legal Values and Correctional Values," *University of Toronto Law Journal* 18 (1968):120–122.

12. K. T. Erikson, *Wayward Puritans* (New York: John Wiley, 1966), pp. 204–205.

13. Howard Levy and David Miller, *Going to Jail: The Political Prisoner* (New York: Grove Press, 1971), p. 103.

14. See, e.g., Francis A. Allen, "The Supreme Court, Federalism, and State Systems of Criminal Justice," *De Paul Law Review* 8 (1959): 212; Yale Kamisar, "Wolf and Lustig Ten Years Later: Illegal State Evidence in State and Federal Courts," *Minnesota Law Review* 43 (1959): 1083; W. V. Schaefer, "Federalism and State Criminal Procedure," *Harv. Law Review* 70 (1956):1.

15. See T. I. Emerson, David Haber, and Norman Dorson, *Political and Civil Rights in the United States,* 3d ed. (Boston: Little, Brown, 1967), I, 104–207.

16. See, e.g., Allen, *Borderland of Criminal Justice;* Norval Morris and Colin Howard, "Penal Sanctions and Human Rights," *Studies in Criminal Law* (London: Oxford, 1964), pp. 147–196; T. S. Szasz, *Psychiatric Justice* (New York: Macmillan, 1965); P. W. Tappan, *Crime, Justice, and Correction* (New York: McGraw-Hill, 1960), pp. 390–395; C. W. Mills, *Power, Politics and People* (New York: Oxford University Press, 1963), pp. 450–452.

17. Cf. June L. Tapp, "Reflections," *Journal of Social Issues* 27, no. 2 (1971):1, 2: "To many liberal psychologists the study of normal behavior in a legal setting suggests a sellout. Many fear their findings may be used by the 'enemy,' i.e., the purveyors of an ideology of repression rather than an ideology of expression." Cf. also the comments of Professor Wolfgang in Jon Snodgrass, "Dialogue with Marvin Wolfgang," *Issues in Criminology* 7 (1972):52–53: "If I have any fear about the subjugation of the scientific spirit, the general imagination of inquiry, it is that the American criminologist will get caught in a process that is forever designed to wipe out and control the phenomenom we call crime. This produces a kind of mechanistic approach to the analysis of crime and criminals. One of the reasons I have an affinity for the current approach in criminology that speaks eloquently about labelling theory and the contribution which the criminal justice systems in general have in the production of crime is that this approach is one that can more critically examine and analyze the system without being married to it. I find this approach not merely a refreshing part of intellectual thought in American sociology and criminology in particular, but it is a return to more purity in intellectual pursuits and scientific analyses."

18. Halleck, *Politics of Therapy,* p. 30.

19. Hermann Mannheim, *Criminal Justice and Social Reconstruction* (New York: Oxford University Press, 1946), p. 1.

20. See also E. M. Schur, *Our Criminal Society* (Englewood Cliffs: Prentice-Hall, 1969), p. 194.

21. In contrast to the modern political awareness and activism, see Aldous Huxley's strictures on the sociology of the last generation: "A senseless world, where nothing whatever can be done—how satisfactory! One can go off and (seeing there's nothing else to do) compile one's treatise on sociology—the science of human senselessness." *Eyless in Gaza* (New York: Harper, 1936), p. 127. For a different emphasis, see E. H. Czajkoski, "A Brief for Public Policy Analysis in Criminological Research," *Criminology* 9 (1971):223.

22. Gene Carte, "Dialogue with Jerome Skolnick," *Issues in Criminology* 4 (1969):118.

23. Louis Proal, *Political Crime* (New York, 1898), p. 99.

24. Isaiah Berlin, "Does Political Theory Still Exist?" in Peter Lassett and W. G. Runciman, eds., *Philosophy, Politics and Society,* 2d ser. (Oxford: Blackwell, 1962), p. 19. Quoted in E. J. Brown, "Quis Custodiet Ipsos Custodes?—The School-Prayer Cases," *Supreme Court Review,* 1963, p. 1.

25. David H. Bayley, "The Police and Political Change in Comparative Perspective," *Law and Society Review* 6 (1971):110. See also John A. Gardiner, "Research Models in Law Enforcement," *Law and Society Review* 6 (1971):229: "I do not in any sense question the duty of the scholar to consider the uses to which his research will be put before he undertakes a project; I only wish to point out that lawyers and social scientists have long claimed an ability to analyze major public issues and policies and should be willing to turn their skills to law enforcement problems."

26. "A large share of the reluctance in liberal circles to explore better ways to combat crime is based on the fear that developments in that area will be used to suppress political dissent as well as illegal behavior." G. M. Sykes, "The Future of Criminality," *American Behavioral Science* 15 (1972):417.

27. D. J. Black, "The Boundaries of Legal Sociology," *Yale Law Journal* 81 (1972):1086.

28. Letter dated Sept. 23, 1860, in M. L. Shuster, ed., *A Treasury of the World's Great Letters* (New York: Simon and Schuster, 1940), p. 343.

29. Cf. Black, "Boundaries of Legal Sociology," p. 1087.

30. Richard Quinney, *The Social Reality of Crime* (Boston: Little, Brown, 1970), pp. 15–18. Quinney stated six propositions (pp. 15–16, 18, 20, 22–23, italics removed): "1 (DEFINITIONS OF CRIME): Crime is a definition of human conduct that is created by authorized agents in a po-

litically organized society . . . 2 (FORMULATION OF CRIMINAL DEFINI-TIONS): Criminal definitions describe behaviors that conflict with the interests of the segments of society that have the power to shape public policy . . . 3 (APPLICATION OF CRIMINAL DEFINITIONS): Criminal definitions are applied by the segments of society that have the power to shape the enforcement and administration of criminal law . . . 4 (DE-VELOPMENT OF BEHAVIOR PATTERNS IN RELATION TO CRIMINAL DEFINI-TIONS): Behavior patterns are structured in segmentally organized society in relation to criminal definitions, and within this context persons engage in activities that have relative probablities of being defined as criminal . . . 5 (CONSTRUCTION OF CRIMINAL CONCEPTIONS): Conceptions of crime are constructed and diffused in the segments of society by various means of communication . . . 6 (THE SOCIAL REALITY OF CRIME): The social reality of crime is constructed by the formulation and application of criminal definitions, the development of behavior patterns related to criminal definitions, and the construction of criminal conceptions.''

31. ''An Act for Regulating Trials in Cases of Treason and Misprison of Treason'' 7 Wm. III, c. 3 (1695).

32. See J. F. Stephen, *A History of the Criminal Law of England* (London, 1883), I, ch. 11; G. L. Haskins, *Law and Authority in Early Massachusetts* (New York: Macmillan, 1960), p. 202.

33. One example is Throckmorton's Case, 1 How. St. Tr. 869 (1544).

34. ''In 1919, the xenophobia common in America before the war was greatly exacerbated, and Palmer, like many others, was caught up in the powerful upsurge of feeling against recent immigrants. He wrote of the alien radicals arrested during the Palmer Raids: 'Out of the sly and crafty eyes of many of them leaped cupidity, cruelty, insanity and crime; from their lopsided faces, sloping brows, and misshapen features may be recognized the unmistakable criminal type.' '' Stanley Coban, *A. Mitchell Palmer: Politician* (New York: Columbia University Press, 1963), p. 198. See also pp. 217–218n46; William Preston, *Aliens and Dissenters* (Cambridge: Harvard University Press, 1963), pp. 7–8.

35. ''In the final analysis, even a subjugated judiciary would have wanted to make its judgments according to the provisions of a clear, written law, not according to telephoned instructions—and even the Nazis could not produce laws fast enough to keep pace with their rapidly changing goals. Hitler soon realized this, and he had a real and deepseated antipathy—often expressed in drastic language—to lawyers, who blocked every undertaking with their documented objections. Here, too, he finally decided to by-pass the judiciary.'' Helmut Krausnick, ''Stages of Coordination,'' in Fritz Stern, ed., *The Path to Dictatorship, 1918–19* (Garden City: Anchor Books, 1966), p. 145.

36. American Law Institute, "Model Penal Code" (Proposed official draft, Philadelphia, 1962); "Recodification of the Criminal Laws," *Journal of Law Reform* 4 (1971):425–485; S. 1, 93d Cong., 1st sess., 1973.

37. Adam Smith, *The Wealth of Nations* (London, 1796), III, 80–81; Joseph Conrad, *The Secret Agent* (Garden City: Doubleday, Page, 1926), p. 173.

38. Jerome Hall, *Theft, Law and Society,* 2d ed. (Indianapolis: Bobbs-Merrill, 1952), pp. 3–142. See also F. A. Allen, "Offenses Against Property," *Annals* 339 (Jan. 1962):58; American Law Institute, "Model Penal Code" (Tentative draft no. 1, 1953), pp. 101–106.

39. See Hall, *Theft, Law and Society,* pp. 114–118; Leon Radzinowicz, *A History of English Criminal Law* (New York: Macmillan, 1948), I, 3–83.

40. Mannheim, *Criminal Justice and Social Reconstruction,* pp. 83–130.

41. Bayley, "The Police and Political Change," p. 103; G. C. Hazard, Book Review, *University of Chicago Law Review* 34 (1966): 229; J. P. Levine, "Implementing Legal Policies Through Operant Conditioning: The Case of Police Practices," *Law and Society Review* 6 (1971):202–205; A. J. Reiss, Jr., *The Police and the Public* (New Haven: Yale University Press, 1971), pp. 127–129, 162, 169, 198–199; J. H. Skolnick, *The Politics of Protest* (New York: Simon and Schuster, 1969), pp. 252, 271, 279–281, 286–287; J. Q. Wilson, *Varieties of Police Behavior* (Cambridge: Harvard University Press, 1968), pp. 230–233.

42. See the definitions of "mental health" in Barbara Wooten *Social Science and Social Pathology* (London: George Allen and Unwin, 1959), pp. 210–221.

43. See, e.g., V. H. Mark and F. R. Ervin, *Violence and the Brain* (New York: Harper and Row, 1970); H. Narabayashi et al., "Stereotaxic Amygdalotomy for Behavior Disorders," *Archives of Neurology,* July 1963, pp. 1–16; R. C. Neville, "Ethical and Philosophical Issues of Behavior Control" (American Association for the Advancement of Science, 139th Meeting, New York, Dec. 27, 1972); "Psychosurgery," *The Lancet,* July 8, 1972, pp. 69–70; "Psychosurgery: Legitimate Therapy or Laundered Lobotomy," *Science* 179 (Mar. 16, 1973): 1109–1111; *The Free World Times* (Minneapolis), Feb. 1972, p. 2; *The Free World Times,* p. 1, cols. 4, 5; Money, "Use of an Androgen-Depleting Hormone in the Treatment of Male Sex Offenders," *Journal of Sex Research* 6 (Aug. 1970):165–172.

2. MISADVENTURES OF A CONCEPT

1. John Harrington, *Epigrams, Of Treason* (1618).

2. Montesquieu, *The Persian Letters,* trans. G. R. Healy, (Indianapolis: Bobbs-Merrill, 1964), p. 174. See also A. E. Evans, "Reflections upon the Political Offense in International Practice," *American Journal of International Law* 21 (1963):57: "In the first place, the concept of the political offense is ambiguous: treason may be justified in terms of high principles of patriotism or condemned as a despicable attack upon the commonwealth itself. *'Les conspirateurs vaincus sont brigandes, victorieux ils sont des héros.'* "

3. See Harry M. Daugherty, "Respect for Law," *A.B.A. Journal* 7:508–509.

4. See, e.g., Council of Europe, *Legal Aspects of Extradition Among European States* (Strasbourg, 1970); Otto Kirchheimer, *Political Justice* (Princeton: Princeton University Press, 1963), pp. 351–388; L. F. L. Oppenheim, *International Law,* vol. I, ed. Hersh Lauterpacht (New York: David McKay, 1955), pp. 705–710; Evans, "Reflections," pp. 1–24.

5. See Treaty of Extradition between the United States and New Zealand, Jan. 12, 1970 (22 UST 1, TIAS 7035). Article VI (4) provides: "Extradition shall not be granted in any of the following circumstances: . . . If the offense for which his extradition is requested is of a political character, or if he proves that the requisition for his surrender has in fact been made with a view to try to punish him for an offense of a political character. If any question arises as to whether a case comes within the provisions of this paragraph, it shall be determined according to the laws of the requested Party."

6. "A critical examination of whether the privilege of the political offender in respect of extradition should be maintained or not, reveals that there are good reasons in its favor. The common crime may generally be considered as harmful and socially dangerous, deserving of punishment, but the political crime is not in itself an action which can justifiably be suppressed. Resistance to a totalitarian regime cannot be reprimanded. Furthermore, if a political offender is surrendered there is the fear that the rulers of the requesting state who have been attacked by the offender may use the criminal proceedings as a pretext for vengeance and for subjecting the accused to unjust and illegal actions. The possibility of this happening is in itself sufficient justification for excluding extradition for political offenses. The surrender of a political offender could also compel the requested state to hand over a person

87

whose sole crime has been an attempt to introduce into the requesting state a political system already adopted by the requested state." Hans Schultz, "The Principles of the Traditional Law of Extradition," in Council of Europe, *Legal Aspects of Extradition,* pp. 15–16.

7. Oppenheim, *International Law,* I, 707–708.

8. Oppenheim, *International Law,* I, 709.

9. See M. R. Garcia-Mora, "Crimes Against Humanity and the Principle of Nonextradition of Political Offenders," *Michigan Law Review* 62 (1964):927.

10. See Kirchheimer, *Political Justice,* pp. 351–365.

11. A "Draft Convention on Terrorism and Kidnapping of Persons for Purposes of Extrosion" was approved by the General Assembly of the Organization of American States on Feb. 2, 1971. The vote was 13–1 with two abstentions. The Preamble notes that "criminal acts against persons entitled to special protection under international law are occurring frequently." One objective of the Convention is the adoption of general standards of international law "as regards cooperation in the prevention and punishment of such acts." *Annals of International Studies, 1972* (Alumni Association, Graduate Institute of International Studies, Geneva), pp. 156–157. See especially the text of the Memorandum of Understanding signed by the United States and Cuba on Feb. 15, 1973; in particular: "The party in whose territory the perpetrators of the acts . . . first arrive may take into consideration any extenuating or mitigating circumstances in those cases in which the persons responsible for the acts were being sought for strictly political reasons and were in real and imminent danger of death without a viable alternative for leaving the country, provided there was no financial extortion or physical injury to the members of the crew, passengers, or other persons in connection with the hijacking." *New York Times,* Feb. 16, 1973, p. 4.

12. See B. L. Ingraham and Kazuhiko Tokaro, "Political Crime in the United States and Japan: A Comparative Study," *Issues in Criminology* 4 (1969): 145–170; Robert Ferrari, "Political Crime," *Columbia Law Review* 20 (1920): 308; Kirchheimer, *Political Justice,* pp. 30–45; J. L. E. Ortolan, *Eléments du droit pénal,* 5th ed. (Paris, 1886), pp. 707–709.

13. Robert Vouin and Jacques Léauté, *Droit pénal et procédure pénale* (Paris: Presses Universitaires, 1969), p. 34.

14. Cesare Lombroso, *Criminal Man* (New York: Putnam, 1911), p. 186. Cf. Raffaele Garofalo, *Criminology,* trans. R. W. Millar (Montclair: Patterson Smith, 1968), p. 217.

15. Ingraham and Takora, "Political Crime," pp. 146–147; Daniel Glaser, "Politicalization of Prisoners: A New Challenge," *Los Angeles Times,* Sept. 19, 1971, Sec. G.

16. Brendan Behan, *Borstal Boy* (New York: Knopf, 1959), p. 287.

Cf. Howard Levy and David Miller, *Going to Jail: The Political Prisoner* (New York: Grove Press, 1971), pp. 194–195: "There is one indication which points to the suspicion that the Bureau of Prisons will not set up camps for the exclusive use of political prisoners. If the government did move in that direction, it would then have to admit the existence of political prisoners, an admission we do not think it is ready to make."

17. See Ingraham and Tokoro, "Political Crime," pp. 147–148, 152–155; Kirchheimer, *Political Justice,* p. 40 ff.

18. It has been asserted that in the 1960s war resisters suffered comparative disadvantages in sentencing and parole in the federal system. Willard Gaylin, *In the Service of Their Country* (New York: Viking, 1970), p. 327; Willard Gaylin, "No Exit," *Harper's,* Nov. 1971, pp. 91–92.

19. N. L. Nathanson, "Freedom of Association and the Quest for Internal Security: Conspiracy from Dennis to Dr. Spock," *Northwestern University Law Review* 65 (1970):153. See also T. I. Emerson, "Freedom of Association and Freedom of Expression," *Yale Law Journal* 74 (1964):1; Elliot Richardson, "Freedom of Expression and the Function of Courts," *Harvard Law Review* 65 (1951):1; Eugene V. Rostow, "The Democratic Character of Judicial Review," *Harvard Law Review* 66 (1952):193.

20. The differences are especially apparent in such areas as sedition-type offenses. See, e.g., André Touleman, ed., *Code de la presse,* 9th ed. (Paris: Libraire Sirey, 1964), pp. 11, 12, 15, 112, 120, 123. Note especially the law of Jan. 5, 1951 (pp. 120–121): "All shouts and chants of a seditious nature voiced in public places or public meetings shall be punished by imprisonment of six days to one month and a fine of 6,000–180,000 Fr. or by one of these sanctions."

21. See Daugherty, "Respect for Law," pp. 509–510.

22. Frank J. Battisti, "The Independence of the Federal Judiciary," *Boston College Industrial and Commercial Law Review* 13 (1972):421.

23. A similar comment can be made about England since the Glorious Revolution. Cf. George Orwell, "The English People" (1947), in Sonia Orwell and Ian Angus, eds., *The Collected Essays, Journalism, and Letters of George Orwell,* (New York: Harcourt, Brace and World, 1968), III, 3: "There is no revolutionary tradition in England, and even in extremist political parties, it is only the middle-class membership that thinks in revolutionary terms. The masses still more or less assume that 'against the law' is a synonym for 'wrong' . . . An Englishman does not believe in his bones, as a Spanish or Italian peasant does, that the law is simply a racket."

24. "In fact a magnificent book could be written on violence in

American life . . . [W]hat can, of course, raise such a book above the level of a mere description of certain sensational aspects of our history is the need to explain why the extraordinary American penchant for violence has been so sporadic, channeled, and controlled that it has usually bled itself out in the isolated, the local, and the partial, instead of coalescing into major political movements." Richard Hofstadter, *The Progressive Historians: Turner, Beard, Parrington* (New York: Random House, 1968), p. 462.

25. The "new penology" can be dated at least from the Declaration of Principles adopted by the Cincinnati Prison Congress of 1870. A condemnation of American prisons written over four decades ago illustrates a criticism that might have been made at any time in the past century: "What monuments to stupidity are these institutions we have built—stupidity not so much of the inmates as of free citizens! What a mockery of science are our prison discipline, our massing of social iniquity in prisons, the good and the bad together in one stupendous *potpourri*. How silly of us to think that we can prepare men for social life by reversing the ordinary process of socialization—silence for the only animal with speech; repressive regimentation of men who are in prison because they need to learn how to exercise their activities in constructive ways; outward conformity to rules which repress all efforts at constructive expressions; work without the operation of economic motives; motivation by fear of punishment rather than hope of reward or appeal to their higher motives; cringing rather than growing in manliness; rewards secured by the betrayal of a fellow rather than by the development of a larger loyalty." John L. Gillin, *Taming the Criminal* (1931), quoted in H. E. Barnes, "The Contemporary Prison: A Menace to Inmate Rehabilitation and the Repression of Crime," *Key Issues* 2 (1965):23. Skepticism and disillusionment had been expressed much earlier: "The theories on the reform of prisoners are vague and uncertain. It is not yet known to what degree the wicked may be regenerated, and by what means this regeneration may be obtained: but if the efficiency of the prisons in correcting prisoners is yet doubtful, its power of depraving them still more is known, because experience proves it." Gustave de Beaumont and Alexis de Tocqueville, *On the Penitentiary System in the United States, and Its Application in France* (Philadelphia, 1833), p. 81. Following is a typical modern statement: "Life in many institutions is at best barren and futile, at worst unspeakably brutal and degrading . . . [T]he conditions in which they [the offenders] live are the poorest possible preparation for their successful re-entry into society, and often merely reinforce in them the pattern of manipulation or destructiveness." Presidents Commission on Law Enforcement and Administration of Justice, *The Challenge of Crime in A Free Society* (Washington, D.C.: U.S. Government Printing Office, 1967), p. 159.

26. George Orwell, *The Road to Wigan Pier* (New York: Berkeley, 1961), p. 127.

27. "The anti-colonial perspective, rather unique when expressed by Malcom X in 1964, now provided many blacks with a structured worldview. For the Black Panther Party, for example, it provided the 'basic definition':

" 'We start with the basic definition: that black people in America are a colonized people in every sense of the term and that white America is an organized Imperialist force holding black people in colonial bondage.' " Jerome Skolnick, *The Politics of Protest* (New York: Simon and Schuster, 1969), p. 149. Note also the reference to the "problems of Amerika's black colonies" in G. L. Jackson, *Soledad Brother: The Prison Letters of George Jackson* (New York: Bantam Book, 1970), p. 30.

28. See Jackson, *Soledad Brother,* p. 31; Daniel Glaser, "Politicalization of Prisoners: A New Challenge," *Los Angeles Times,* Sept. 19, 1971, Sec. G; R. K. Baker, "Trends to Radicalization," *Chicago Sun-Times,* Nov. 4, 1971, Sec. 2, p. 3; Ralph de Toledando, "New Left Plans Convict 'Liberation,' " *Jefferson City* [*Mo.*] *News-Tribune,* Oct. 12, 1971; "Prisoner Power: A Radical Turn," *Newsweek,* Sept. 27, 1971, p. 38. See also Gaylin, *In the Service,* p. 308.

29. Norval Morris, "Corrections Lurches Forward" (Address given at the National Conference on Corrections, Williamsburg, Va., Dec. 6, 1971).

30. Philip Berrigan, *Prison Journals of a Priest Revolutionary* (New York: Holt, Rinehart and Winston, 1970), p. 35. See also Levy and Miller, *Going to Jail,* p. xi: "Of course, the vast majority of inmates in American prisons are political prisoners in the wider sense of the word. Prisons reflect the class bias of the society which they serve, and the inmates are its victims."

31. Cf. Daniel Glaser, "The Sociological Approach to Crime and Corrections," *Law and Contemporary Problems* 23 (1958):683; S. L. Messinger, "Issues in the Study of the Social System of Prison Inmates," *Issues in Criminology* 4 (1969):136.

32. See, e.g., M. E. Wolfgang, R. M. Figlie, and Thorsten Sellin, *Delinquency in a Birth Cohort,* Studies in Crime and Justice (Chicago: University of Chicago Press, 1972).

33. Clark Hoyt, "Attica Boss Blasts Negotiations," *Detroit Free Press,* Nov. 30, 1971, p. 5-B. Clark Hoyt, "Attica Warden, Prison Chief Split," *Detroit Free Press,* Dec. 1, 1971, p. 5-B.

34. Margaret Mead, *Culture and Commitment* (Garden City: Doubleday, 1970), p. 67.

35. Cf. E. M. Forster, *Two Cheers for Democracy* (New York: Harcourt, Brace and World, 1951), p. 14: "To me, anti-Semitism is now the most shocking of all things. It is destroying much more than the

Jews; it is assailing the human mind at its source, and inviting it to create false categories before exercising judgment.''

36. ''Henry Cockburn, a nineteenth century Scottish lawyer handling political trials and later a judge, used the following characterization: 'To see no difference between political and other offenses is the sure mark of an excited or stupid head' (*An Examination of the Trials for Sedition in Scotland,* Edinburgh, 1888 [written in 1853], Vol. 1, p. 68).'' Kirchheimer, *Political Justice,* p. 48n2.

37. Cf. Michael Barkun, ''Law and Social Revolution: Millenarianism and the Legal System,'' *Law and Society Review* 6 (1971):128–129: ''The rule systems that operate within revolutionary movements do not observe conventional distinctions between public and private, religious and secular, political and non-political, belief and behavior. Depending on how one wishes to view it, everything is political or nothing . . . hence 'minor' crimes—petty thievery, for example, are elevated to the status of capital offenses . . . and, of course, doctrinal deviations become matters of central judicial concern.''

38. 468 F.2d. 141, 148 (7 Cir. 1972).

39. See Herbert L. Packer, ''Offenses Against the State,'' *Annals of the American Academy of Political and Social Science* 339 (Jan. 1962):77.

40. See W. L. Shirer, *The Rise and Fall of the Third Reich* (New York: Simon and Schuster, 1960), pp. 188–195. The case illustrates difficulties in the proposed classification. Viewed simply as a trumped-up charge of arson, the proceeding falls within the second category. However, as the defendants were charged with the destruction of interests that could surely be described as political, the case falls as easily within the first category.

41. See, e.g., H. B. Ehrmann, *The Untried Case* (New York: Vanguard, 1933); O. K. Fraenkel, *The Sacco-Vanzetti Case* (New York: Knopf, 1931); G. L. Joughin and E. M. Morgan, *The Legacy of Sacco and Vanzetti* (New York: Harcourt, Brace, 1948).

42. Cf. C. R. Ashman, *The People v. Angela Davis* (New York: Pinnacle Books, 1972), pp. 162–166.

43. Cf. Nathan Hackman, ''Political Trials in the Legal Order: A Political Scientist's Perspective,'' *Journal of Public Law* 21 (1972):125: ''Such ideological or institutional 'crimes' may be treated in the context of social and economic warfare and treated differently from private acts of passion or other more idiosyncratic types of individual offenses.''

44. See United States v. Moylan, 417 F.2d 1002 (4th Cir. 1969), cert. denied 397 U.S. 910 (1970), in which the court held that appellants were not entitled to an instruction informing the jury that it had power to disregard the law as defined by the trial judge. Cf. Joseph L. Sax, ''Conscience and Anarchy: The Prosecution of War Resisters,'' *The Yale Review* 57 (1968):481.

3. REFLECTIONS ON THE TRIALS OF OUR TIME

1. Otto Kirchheimer, *Political Justice* (Princeton: Princeton University Press, 1961), p. ix; Brown v. United States, 256 U.S. 335, 343 (1921).

2. An exception is P.L. 92–128, 92d Cong., 1st Sess., 85 Stat. 347 (1971), which *inter alia* repealed Title II of the Internal Security Act of 1950 (50 U.S.C. 811–826). Title II related to the "Emergency Detention of Suspected Security Risks" and, subject to certain conditions, authorized the establishment of detention camps.

3. The field of alien deportation during the early years of the century is an example. Beginning with the Immigration Act of 1903, Congress added increasingly broad grounds for the exclusion and deportation of aliens, relating especially to matters of belief and association. Although not hitherto used extensively for the deportation of radical aliens, the legislation was available for such use during the postwar hysteria, most notably for the arrests and deportations associated with the Palmer Raids of 1919 and 1920. Although the raids produced shock and public reexamination of administrative procedures, the main thrust of the legislation was not deflected and was, in fact, strengthened in subsequent enactments. See William Preston, Jr., *Aliens and Dissenters* (Cambridge: Harvard University Press, 1963); R. K. Murray, *Red Scare* (Minneapolis: University of Minnesota Press, 1955).

4. 1 Stat. 112 (1st Cong., 2d Sess., 1790).

5. Kirchheimer, *Political Justice,* p. 419.

6. Cf. E. A. Kent, *Revolution and the Rule of Law* (Englewood Cliffs: Prentice-Hall, 1971), p. 10: "Short of a full revolutionary stance that denies all legitimacy to the legal system, equal punishment for serious crimes seems a rooted and universal standard of justice."

7. "They had yielded to the propaganda, widespread in both political and legal circles, that believing oneself to have acted in the national interest, if it does not justify assassination, at least exculpates it. These groups were the first to regret bitterly that they ever allowed themselves to embrace a thesis whose logical extension led a few years later to the generalized murder of inconvenient political adversaries under the National Socialist regime." Kirchheimer, *Political Justice,* p. 413.

8. See Richard Hammer, *The Court-Martial of Lieutenant Calley* (New York: Coward, McCann & Geoghegan, 1971).

9. For evidence of new interest and concern, see F. E. Zimring and G. J. Hawkins, *Deterrence: The Legal Threat in Crime Control* (Chicago: University of Chicago Press, 1973); S. H. Kadish, "Some Observations on the Use of Criminal Sanctions in Enforcing Economic Regu-

lations," *University of Chicago Law Review* 30 (1963): 423; H. V. Ball and L. M. Friedman, "Use of Criminal Sanctions in Enforcing Economic Legislation: A Sociological View," *Stanford Law Review* 17 (1965): 197.

10. "It must be admitted, of course, that these uses of penal provisions are highly dependent upon the political balance of power, and on many other circumstances. During an enemy occupation threat of punishment against traitors will have little weight for those who feel certain that the occupier will win the war. And in certain cases—e.g., after a civil war—it can happen that prosecution of the rebels will not increase respect for a state's authority, but indeed perpetuate a split, in a way that can have serious repercussions. In such cases it can become difficult for the law makers to decide which is wiser; to overlook the crime by resorting to a partial or general amnesty, or to hold the guilty ones responsible to the fullest extent of the law." Johannes Andenaes, "General Prevention—Illusion or Reality?" *Journal of Criminal Law, Criminology, and Police Science* 3 (1952):190.

11. Cf. E. M. Schur, *Our Criminal Society* (Englewood Cliffs: Prentice-Hall, 1969), p. 225: "There is no evidence to indicate that legislation aimed at nebulously defined 'subversive' activity has ever had any significant value in promoting the general welfare in a democratic society."

12. Jason Epstein, *The Great Conspiracy Trial* (New York: Vintage Books, 1970), pp. 100–101; Murray, *Red Scare,* pp. 30–31, 272–273; Preston, *Aliens,* pp. 122, 127–128, 150–151.

13. "But of all the effects of the Red Scare on the life of the 1920's, probably none was more striking than the impact on the domestic radical movement itself. As a result of the Scare hysteria, the two Communist factions were driven completely underground where they found it increasingly difficult to publicize the Communist movement." Murray, *Red Scare,* p. 276.

14. "If, however, the main purpose of the trial was to prevent draft resistance and its adult support, the effect produced was exactly the opposite." J. H. Skolnick, *The Politics of Protest* (New York: Simon and Schuster, 1969), p. 73.

15. See, e.g., Epstein, *Great Conspiracy Trial;* J. A. Lukas, *The Barnyard Epithet and Other Obscenties* (New York: Harper and Row, 1970); M. L. Levine, G. C. McNamee, and Daniel Greenberg, *The Tales of Hoffman* (New York: Bantam Books, 1970).

16. For an account of the trial, see Raymonds Wills, "Love on Trial: The Berrigan Case Reconsidered," *Harper's,* July 1972, p. 63.

17. Illinois Unified Code of Corrections, Public Act 77-2097 (1972).

18. See Murray, *Red Scare,* pp. 195–196; Stanley Coban, *A. Mitchell Palmer: Politician* (New York: Columbia University Press, 1963).

19. See Preston, *Aliens,* pp. 7–8.

20. Cf. K. T. Erikson, *Wayward Puritans* (New York: Wiley, 1966), pp. 8–19.

21. *The Letters of the Younger Pliny,* trans. Betty Radice, (London: Penguin Books, 1971), Book Ten, no. 96, pp. 293–294; no. 97, p. 295.

22. See Epstein, *Great Conspiracy Trial,* pp. 6–7. Cf. the remarks of the United States Circuit Court in the Chicago Seven case: ''The district judge's deprecatory and often antagonistic attitude toward the defense is evident in the record from the very beginning. It appears in remarks and actions both in the presence and absence of the jury . . . Most significant, however, were remarks in the presence of the jury, deprecatory of defense counsel and their case. These comments were often touched with sarcasm, implying rather than saying outright that defense counsel was inept, bumptious, or untrustworthy, or that his case lacked merit.'' United States v. Dellinger, 472 F.2d 340, 386, 387 (7th Cir. 1972).

23. See Louis Proal, *Political Crime* (New York, 1898), p. 296.

24. See C. B. Cone, *The English Jacobins: Reformers in the Late Eighteenth Century* (New York: Charles Scribner's Sons, 1968), p. 174.

25. John Bullock, *Akin to Treason* (London: Arthur Baker, 1966), pp. 24–25; Rosenberg v. United States, 195 F.2d 583 (2d Cir. 1952).

26. ''But the greatest and the most intangible risk for a constitutional government does not lie in the ever-present possibility that a prosecution might presently backfire and bring its promoters a measure of legal and political discomfiture. Its greatest risk might be called the historical risk.'' Kirchheimer, *Political Justice,* pp. 198–199.

27. Gresham Sykes and David Matza, ''Techniques of Neutralization: A Theory of Delinquency,'' *American Sociological Review* 22 (1957):664.

28. David M. Potter, ''Changing Patterns of Social Cohesion and the Crisis of Law under a System of Government by Consent,'' in E. V. Rostow, ed., *Is Law Dead?* (New York: Simon and Schuster, 1971), p. 283.

29. Philip Berrigan, *Prison Journals of a Priest Revolutionary* (New York: Holt, Rinehart and Winston, 1970), pp. 111, 103.

30. Richard Quinney, *The Social Reality of Crime* (Boston: Little, Brown, 1970), pp. 258–259.

31. In no modern case has the government suffered so complete a reversal of its role from accuser to accused as in the prosecution of Daniel Ellsberg.

32. Theodore Mommsen, *Remisches Strafrecht,* quoted in Kirchheimer, *Political Justice,* p. 304.

33. ''Impartiality presupposes a commonly accepted starting proposition.'' Kirchheimer, *Political Justice,* p. 215.

34. The so-called Camden 28 trial, in which the accused were charged with offenses relating to breaking and entering a selective service office with intent to destroy draft records, was apparently characterized by more than ordinary permissiveness on the part of the trial judge toward defense efforts to communicate defendants' motives in committing the crimes. The case was also remarkable for the degree of participation of federal undercover agents in planning and executing the offense. Judge Clarkson S. Fisher instructed that the federal laws could not properly be nullified because the jury agreed with the defendants about the Indochinese war, but left to the jury the question as to whether in its undercover activity the government had gone to lengths "offensive to basic standards of decency and shocking to the universal sense of justice." The defendants were acquitted. See "Political Trials," *The Nation,* June 4, 1973, pp. 708–709.

35. 347 U.S. 483 (1954).

36. Omnibus Crime Control and Safe Streets Act of 1968, 82 Stat. 197.

37. Dellinger v. United States, 472 F.2d 340 (7th Cir. 1972); United States v. Spock, 416 F.2d 165 (1st Cir. 1969).

38. C. R. Ashman, *The People v. Angela Davis* (New York: Pinnacle Books, 1972), p. 158.

39. See A.B.A. Project on Standards for Criminal Justice, *The Prosecution Function and the Defense Function* (Tentative Draft, 1970), p. 92: "In cases which involve a serious threat to the community, the prosecutor should not be deterred from prosecution by the fact that in his jurisdiction juries have tended to acquit persons accused of the particular kind of criminal act in question."

40. Robert H. Jackson, "The Federal Prosecutor," *Journal of Criminal Law and Criminology* 31 (1940):5; Kirchheimer, *Political Justice,* p. 196n41.

41. See Epstein, *Great Conspiracy Trial,* pp. 33–34. One defendant, Rennie Davis, was quoted as saying: "In choosing the eight of us, the government has lumped together all the strands of dissent in the 60's." Lucas, *Barnyard Epithet,* p. 2.

42. Cf. J. T. Elliff, *Crime, Dissent, and the Attorney General* (Beverly Hills: Sage Publications, 1971), p. 187.

43. See, e.g., Jessica Mitford, *The Trial of Doctor Spock* (New York: Knopf, 1970), p. 56.

44. Johannes Andenaes, "The General Preventive Effects of Punishment," *University of Pennsylvania Law Review* 114 (1966):942, 181–183.

45. To surcharge the system was declared a deliberate purpose by one of the defendants in the Spock case. Faber, "On Being Indicted," in *Trials of the Resistance* (New York: New York Review of Books,

1970), p. 47. See also Kirchheimer, *Political Justice,* pp. 160–161, 171–172.

46. See, e.g., Dixon v. District of Columbia, 394 F.2d 966 (D.C. Cir. 1968); People v. Gray, 254 Cal. App. 2d 256, 63 Cal. Rptr. 211 (1967).

47. "Because their experience and training encourage them to define problems according to the facts of specific cases, Department lawyers tend to conceive policy issues in terms of particular prosecutions and lawsuits. While this has the advantage of compelling executives to concentrate on the immediate effects of their decisions, it hampers their ability to develop larger policy goals." Elliff, *Crime,* p. 8.

48. See K. C. Davis, *Discretionary Justice* (Baton Rouge: Louisiana State University Press, 1969), pp. 224–225.

49. The press reported approval by the President in July 1970 of a secret White House intelligence plan, reputedly written by Tom Charles Huston. One of the documents approved, entitled "Recommendations: Operational Restraints in Intelligence Collection," included the following: "Surreptitious Entry. Recommendation: Present restrictions should be modified to permit procurement of vitally needed foreign cryptographic material. Also, present restrictions should be modified to permit selective use against other urgent security targets.

"Rationale: Use of this technique is clearly illegal. It amounts to burglary. It is also highly risky and could result in great embarrassment if exposed. However it is also the most fruitful tool and can produce the type of intelligence which cannot be obtained in any other fashion . . .

"Surreptitious entry of facilities occupied by subversive elements can turn up information about identities, methods of operation, and other invaluable investigative information which is not otherwise obtainable. This technique would be particularly helpful if used against the Weathermen and Black Panthers." *Chicago Tribune,* June 10, 1973, Sec. 2, p. 1. Huston was quoted in the same issue (p. 2): "The real threat to internal security—in any society—is repression . . . But repression is an inevitable result of disorder. Forced to choose between order and freedom, people will take order. A handful of people can't frontally overthrow the government . . . But if they can engender enough fear, they can generate an atmosphere that will bring out of the woodwork every repressive demagog in the country. Unless this stuff was stopped, the country was going to fall into the wrong hands."

If this language is accepted at face value, it shows that Huston had become part of a repression he purported to loathe. Clearly, also, his sophistication was insufficient to encompass the elementary historical perception that in advocating the use of repression to avoid repression, he was advancing a classic version of the tyrant's plea.

50. One important incident of this kind involved the so-called Media

papers. In March 1971 there was a theft of files from a small FBI office in Media, Pennsylvania. Shortly thereafter a group acting under the name Commission to Investigate the FBI distributed to major newspapers quantities of documents said to have been copied from the stolen files. The papers appeared to support charges of infiltration of various groups, including college campuses. One paper, purporting to be an internal memorandum, proposed a program to intensify the "paranoia" that there was "an FBI agent behind every mailbox." Jack Nelson and R. J. Ostrow, *The FBI and the Berrigans* (New York: Coward, McCann & Geoghegan, 1972), pp. 186–188. See also *New York Times* 7 (Mar. 10, 1971):1; 24 (Mar. 24, 1972):3; *New Republic* 164 (Apr. 10, 1971):5–7; (May 1, 1971):9–10; *Time* 97 (Apr. 5, 1971):15.

51. See Harry Kalven, " 'Please, Morris, Don't Make Trouble': Two Lessons in Courtroom Confrontation," *Journal of Social Issues* 27 (1971):229–230; United States v. McWilliams, 54 F. Supp. 791 (D.D.C. 1944); 163 F.2d 695 (D.C. Cir. 1947).

52. Judge Coffin's comment in his dissent in the Spock case is persuasive: "The court's action underscores my conviction that in the First Amendment area finely honed distinctions do not serve as effective safeguards because they do not provide a basis for prediction of the legal consequences of future conduct." 416 F.2d 165, 191 (1st Cir. 1969).

53. See Elliff, *Crime,* p. 244.

54. See, e.g., A. R. Miller, *The Assault on Privacy* (Ann Arbor: University of Michigan Press, 1971).

55. Bruce Smith, *Police Systems in the United States* (New York: Harper, 1949), pp. 10–11.

56. See, e.g., John Kaplan, *Marijuana: The New Prohibition* (New York: World, 1970); Norval Morris and Gordon Hawkins, *The Honest Politician's Guide to Crime Control* (Chicago: University of Chicago Press, 1970); H. L. Packer, *The Limits of the Criminal Sanction* (Stanford: Stanford University Press, 1968); John Junker, "Criminalization and Criminogenesis," *U.C.L.A. Law Review* 19 (1972):697; S. H. Kadish, "The Crisis of Overcriminalization," *Annals* 374 (1967):157; Jerome Skolnick, "Coercion to Virtue: The Enforcement of Morals, *Southern California Law Review* 41 (1968):588.

57. Max Radin, "Enemies of Society," *Journal of Criminal Law and Criminology* 27 (1937):801.

58. *New York Daily News,* Sept. 15, 1971, p. 1; *New York Times,* Sept. 17, 1971, p. 31.

59. Cf. Lankford v. Gelston, 364 F.2d 197 (4th Cir. 1966).

60. "Citizens enter the criminal-justice system not only as violators, but more importantly as enforcers of the law. Their discretionary decisions to mobilize the police are a principal source of input into the sys-

tem, and these decisions profoundly affect the discretion exercised by the police.'' A. J. Reiss, Jr., *The Police and the Public* (New Haven: Yale U. Press, 1971), pp. 114–115; see also pp. 11, 69–70, 105, 108–109, 112–113, 173.

61. See, e.g., D. J. Bordua and L. L. Tifft, ''Citizen Interviews, Organized Feedback, and Police-Community Relations Decisions,'' *Law and Society Review* 2 (1971):165: ''This kind of aggressive-preventive patrol involving search, then, seems to be a particularly costly tactic when employed with blacks. They are *more* likely to think negatively of it, *more* likely to see it as a raw exercise of power, *more* likely to be upset and angry about [the] incident, and *more* likely to see race prejudice as involved.''

62. Bertrand Russell, *Power* (New York: Norton, 1938), p. 104.

Index

Aliens. *See* Deportation; Palmer Raids; Political crime
Altgeld, Governor Peter: on Haymarket Case, 58, 59
Amnesty: of Southern adherents after Civil War, 25; pardon of I.W.W. leaders, 52
Andenaes: on deterrent consequences of political prosecutions, 52
Aristotle, 1
Atomic energy: cause of concern about uses of knowledge, 12

Bayley, David H.: on police research, 13
Beals, R. L.: on politics and social science, 3
Behan, Brendan: on political prisoners, 29-30
Berlin, Isaiah, 12
Bernstein, Leonard, 36, 37
Berrigan, Father Philip: futility of the Harrisburg prosecution, 54; on defense tactics in political trials, 60; motivation for the Harrisburg prosecution, 64
Bill of Rights. *See* Constitutional Law
Black, Donald, 14
Black militancy: impact on criminology, 9, 10; produced public discussion of political crime, 26; use of colonial analogy, 35; black inmates as political prisoners, 36
Brown v. School Board: as a source of judicial activism, 62
Burke, Edmund, 65

Busing controversy: proposals for limiting judicial powers, 62

Calley, Lieutenant William L.: public reactions to military prosecution, 49, 50
Camus, Albert: on politics and literature, 3
Casement, Roger: sentence to death, 59
Chase v. United States, 42
Chicago Seven Case: effects on polarization of American society, 53; revealed vulnerability of courts to disruption, 60; reversal of convictions, 63; selection of defendants for, 64, 65; as example of the inutility of mass political trials, 70
Cockburn, Henry: on political prosecutions, 64
Congress of Vienna: period of political repression following, 67
Conrad, Joseph, 19, 20
Conspiracy. *See* Political prosecution
Constitutional law: rights derived from political experience, 4; rights of free speech, 8; doctrines relating to criminal justice, 8; function in political crimes area, 31
Corrections: scarcity of therapeutic programs, 6; role of therapeutic programs in prisons, 8, 10; abusive uses of surgery and drugs, 22, 23; persistence of the American prison problem, 35; prisons as a focal point of agitation, 35; public resistance to

ment, 52, 53; Senate resolution urging action against radicals, 54, 55
Pliny (the Younger): on repression of Christians, 58
Police: as subject of criminological inquiry, 13, 14; departmental control of subordinates, 21; as independent political force, 21, 22; as instrumentality of socially dominant groups, 21, 22; fanaticism in undercover agencies, 68; untrammeled volition of undercover agencies, 68; dangers to political values in the surveillance function, 68, 69; law enforcement abuse as encouragement of political extremism, 69; effect of traffic violations on public support of police function, 73; activity reflecting "war theory" of law enforcement, 75; "aggressive patrol" as threat to individual rights, 75, 76
Political asylum. *See* Extradition
Political crime: infrequent reference to, in public discussions, 25, 26; absence of a doctrine in Anglo-American law, 25, 30-35 *passim,* 46; in the law of extradition, 26-28; definitions, 26, 42, 43-46, 48, 72; "crimes against humanity" doctrine, 27; Continental legal doctrines of mitigation, 28-30, 46; political offenders different from ordinary criminals, 24, 29, 59, 60; First Amendment law as substitute for political crime doctrine, 31; reasons for failing to develop a legal doctrine of, in the United States, 31-35 *passim;* hostility of American lawyers to the concept, 32, 40; American hostility to civil disobedience, 33, 34; utility of the concept, 39-43 *passim;* use of the concept for propaganda purposes, 40-42; inadequacy of the label, 41, 42; usefulness of concept for policy studies, 43; marijuana violations as examples of, 46, 48, 73; role of academic criticism, 47, 48; legislation often the product of hysteria, 47, 48; common feature of

organized society, 48, 49; necessity and inevitability of prosecution, 49, 50, 51, 69, 70; danger of repression to stability of governments, 50, 67; policy questions relating to, 51; difficulties in appraising consequences of policy, 51, 52; as the product of dangerous aliens, 56, 57; political justice is essentially unruly, 67; measures required for reform of the law, 70-71; impossibility of confining attitudes and procedures to political cases, 71; "political" element volatile and expansible, 72; relations to ordinary crimes, 71-77 *passim;* confined by the principle of strict necessity, 76, 77
Political prisoner, 8, 34; black inmates as, 36, 37, 38; ordinary offenders as, 36-39 *passim;* label as obstacle to reform, 38, 39; function of label for protesting groups, 39; reality of, 41
Political prosecution, 34; as a moderation of political oppression, 17-18; necessity and inevitability of, 49, 50, 51, 69, 70; as a threat to the stability of governments, 50, 67; problems of conspiracy cases, 51, 54, 63, 65, 70; selection of defendants for, 51, 65, 66; conviction and imprisonment of I.W.W. leaders, 52; special problems of deterrent consequences, 52; effect on American radical movement, 52, 53; employed to achieve governmental purposes, 52-54, 70; effect of Spock prosecution on draft law violations, 53; effects of the Chicago Seven case, 53; effects of the Philip Berrigan prosecution, 54; induced by public demand, 54, 55, 58; immediate gains may override long-term values, 54, 69, 70; inhibitions on the use of, 55; uncertain public reactions to, 55; unintended consequences of, 55-62 *passim,* 70; failure to perceive changing character of the radical movement, 56; limited success of re-